AMERICA, LET ME IN

A CHOOSE YOUR IMMIGRATION STORY

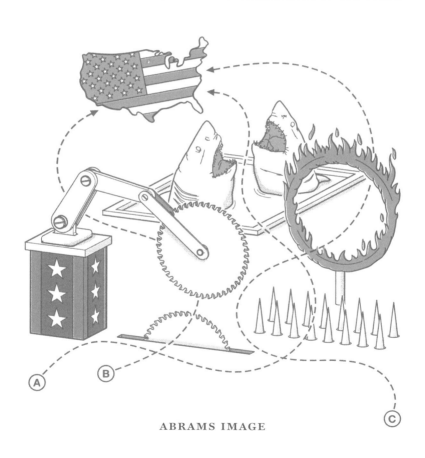

ABRAMS IMAGE

To my mom, who made my American Dream come true.

To my siblings, may this help you see that
the journey is always worth it.

To Taylor, for making this country my home.

CONTENTS

Introduction..1
A Quick Legal Note..5
The Rules of the Game..7
Select a Difficulty Level...9
    Easy...11
    Medium...13
    Hard..37
    Very Hard...187
Why Even Move to America? A Sort-of Conclusion.........189
List of Immigration Terms..195

Acknowledgments..199
About the Author..203

INTRODUCTION

Welcome to *America, Let Me In: A Choose Your Immigration Story*. This book, and its properties, *America, Let Me In: A Choose Your Immigration Movie*; *America, Let Me In: The Ride featuring The Minions*; *America, Let Me In: A Choose Your Song Karaoke Machine*; and *America, Let Me In: A Choose Your Cold Cuts Delicatessen & Bodega* will hopefully serve as the ultimate guide for any person who is curious about what it's like to be an immigrant who dares take on the daunting task of leaving it all behind and moving to a country they picked.

That's the gist of immigrants, by and large. They chose this place. And I believe there is no bigger act of love than willingly choosing something. We only choose the things that we actively want. The things we love. We choose our romantic partners and our pets. Unless you're one of those annoying people who say "actually, he chose *me*" when talking about your dog, which, as much of an idealist and a dog lover as I am, is not true. A dog didn't choose you; at best it chose the residue smell from the bacon you had for breakfast the morning you went to the shelter.

Most Americans have no idea how much work it takes to come to the United States. To become an immigrant. To choose to live here. This book will hopefully give them a chance to learn while also giving them the gift of choosing the United States. It will also try to show many of the incredibly complicated and challenging and expensive ways in which people try to come here. Which, as a fellow immigrant, fulfills my true goal with this book: world domination and the establishment of a global theocracy that venerates Garfield, the cat. No, wait. Sorry. I meant: telling a bunch of stories about immigrants. As living here, or attempting to live here, gets harder for people not born here, I believe it's more important than ever to tell our stories.

If you're an immigrant reading this, first of all, hi! It's so fucking hard, isn't it? I love you. Second of all, I think there should be more books about us. I think there should be more movies and TV shows about us. They say that in America, every person's story gets told. But based on the stuff that gets made, the stories that get told are the ones of every startup founder who goes crazy after inventing something like Tinder for cats. I want our stories to be told. And ideally sold to a Hollywood studio in a multimillion-dollar deal that adapts it into an Emmy Award–winning miniseries on HBO, or Netflix, or QueenView, the new streaming service from Dairy Queen. If Queen-View hasn't been invented by the time you read this book, just wait a couple of years.

That's why I wrote a book where you get to choose America and, also, one where you get to live many immigrant stories, which will all involve some of the many kinds of visas you can acquire in order to move to America. This book does not include *all* the kinds of visas you can get to move to the US. If it did, it would be much longer and much more boring. I tried to focus on visas that allow people to move to the United States and not stuff like the R-1 Temporary Religious Worker visa. To get that visa, a prospective or existing US employer must file Form I-129, Petition for a Nonimmigrant Worker, on behalf of a noncitizen seeking to enter the United States as a non-immigrant minister, or a religious worker in a religious vocation or WAIT WAIT! Don't shut the book, it gets better! I was just proving a point and saying that I tried to pick visas and stories that won't put you to sleep, but also the ones that won't give you nightmares.

That said, I do want to make a couple of things clear: Most of the stories in this book are fictional. I made them up. I can do that because I was blessed by the muses and because I spent way too much of my parents' money on an artistic education. However, some of the stories you will find here are true. They are things that happened to the writer, i.e., me, Felipe Torres Medina. As the sole author of this book, I cannot claim every immigrant narrative as my own, but I can do my best to bring them to light. And I can also do my best to write some jokes at the expense of our ridiculous immigration system.

I know what you're thinking: Jokes? Isn't immigration this big, scary thing that makes the people on the news turn red, like a boiled ham having a heart attack? Yes. But isn't facing daunting, horrible things with optimism and positivity America's whole deal? It certainly was Benjamin Franklin's whole deal. That and French prostitutes. So not to worry, we're going to do this together. And to make sure you stay engaged and really listen to these stories, I'm putting them in a format that will force you to become invested. *You* are the main character. And unlike your friend who thinks he's the main character all the time, you're doing it in a non-annoying way! These stories will become your stories. You will make the choices that will lead you to this country. *America, Let Me In* is a great adventure full of quests, long lines, romance, long lines, thrills, long lines, dragons (there are no dragons), and long lines! And this odyssey is now yours!

Now, as the great American poet will.i.am would say: let's get it started.

》》 CONTINUE TO THE NEXT PAGE 》》

A QUICK LEGAL NOTE

Because this book will deal with immigration, which is an extremely complex issue full of legal ramifications, the very cool and very handsome lawyers who advised me during the writing process have asked me to include a series of disclaimers about the contents of the book. I have included them, but also translated them from legalese. So, here goes:

1. "This publication contains the opinions and ideas of its author. It is sold with the understanding that neither the author nor the publisher is engaged in rendering legal or other professional advice or services. If the reader requires such advice or services, a professional should be consulted." *That means, please do not use this book in lieu of an immigration lawyer. Or any kind of lawyer. I have it on good authority this book did not pass the bar.*

2. "The names of some real people and companies appear in this book, but they are used in an entirely fictitious

manner." That one's pretty straightforward, but yeah. If I mentioned your name in the book, it's all a biting satire that will be recognized either now or in the future as a masterpiece.

Also, throughout the book, you may find some footnotes written by our legal assistant, Kevin. Say hello, Kevin.

Hello.

You seem reticent?

Well, I didn't think I was gonna have to be in the book . . . also, I'm shy.

Well, you asked me to clarify when certain parts of the book are jokes, and I have no interest in ruining my own jokes by adding "(this is a joke)" after them.

So now I have to ruin your jokes?

No. No, you are doing your job: being a boring lawyer. I am doing my job: writing funny things.

Do I get to tell a joke?

No! Write your own joke book on the US immigration system!

THE RULES
OF THE GAME

You are about to embark on an adventure unlike any you can possibly imagine. This adventure will not have hobbits or wizards, but there'll definitely be trolls and scrolls. So many, many scrolls of paperwork. Really, get ready to fill out so many forms. However, before our quest can begin, here are some ground rules:

1. This is going to be fun. There are many, many, way too many immigration stories full of very real pain and suffering. In fact, most immigrant stories involve some level of that. However, what you will not find in this book are the very real cases of violence, extreme poverty, and abuse that many immigrants experience all over the world, on a daily basis. These stories are important and should be told, but they should be told with the grace and care that a joke book with multiple endings and a page ranting about *SpongeBob* cannot give them.

2. If you die in this book, you DO NOT die in real life. This is a fun book, and death is—according to most Yelp reviews—not fun.
3. If you don't like this book, you support ICE.
4. Sorry, I don't make the rules.
5. I absolutely make the rules.

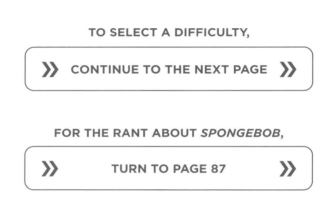

TO SELECT A DIFFICULTY,

» CONTINUE TO THE NEXT PAGE »

FOR THE RANT ABOUT *SPONGEBOB*,

» TURN TO PAGE 87 »

SELECT A
DIFFICULTY LEVEL

Because this is a game, you can also select a difficulty level that will dictate how hard your legal immigration path will be. In real immigration, you don't get to do this. But in this book, you do! If you're an American, you get a choice because you're the specialest, most bestest person on Earth. If you're an immigrant, you get a choice because you've already dealt with enough bullshit in this lifetime.

TO COME TO AMERICA THE "EASY" WAY,

● **TURN TO PAGE 11** ●

TO COME TO AMERICA THE "MEDIUM" WAY,

■ **TURN TO PAGE 13** ■

TO COME TO AMERICA THE "HARD" WAY,

◆ **TURN TO PAGE 37** ◆

TO COME TO AMERICA THE "VERY HARD" WAY,

★ **TURN TO PAGE 187** ★

EASY

Incorrect! There is no easy way to move to America. Your journey has ended before it began!

THE END

- ● RETURN TO PAGE 9 ●

MEDIUM

Your journey begins in your beautiful apartment in the 7th arrondissement of Paris. Of course you live in Paris in a very well-to-do area. You are, after all, a person whose immigration adventure will be medium-level difficult. Life is, undeniably, pretty good. You open your eyes and slowly get out of bed, gently allowing the 900-thread-count sheets to slither down your perfectly sculpted body. Did I mention you're hot? You're super-hot. That also makes your life a little easier.

You stretch, still a little woozy after a night of wining, dining, and incredible sexing with your equally hot partner, and take a look in the mirror.

IF, UPON SEEING YOUR REFLECTION, YOU SEE A GORGEOUS WHITE MAN WITH SALT-AND-PEPPER HAIR, PERFECTLY SCULPTED CHEEKBONES, AND A CHARMING SMILE,

■ TURN TO PAGE 14 ■

IF, UPON SEEING YOUR REFLECTION, YOU SEE AN ELEGANT WOMAN WHOSE HAIR "JUST FRICKING LOOKS LIKE THAT, HOLY SHIT, CAN YOU BELIEVE IT?"

■ TURN TO PAGE 22 ■

■

UPON SEEING YOUR REFLECTION, YOU SEE A GORGEOUS WHITE MAN.

A sudden realization comes to you: Your name is Alexandre Maxime Bouffant de la Fantine Cosette and you're one of the heads of marketing at the top luxury brand in all of France—Louis Vuitton Moët Hennessy Disneyland Paris. But why do you have a nagging feeling that it's important that you remember that? You don't shower because your hair just looks like *that*, and you naturally don't sweat. Also, your beard is scruffy but in a way that makes you look cool, not unkempt.

You have breakfast (coffee, black; cigarettes, white with little orange bit) at an al fresco table at a café in Saint Germain. Then, you remember why it was important you remember your job: you have to go to it! You check GreveHub, the app every French person has on their phone to see if they're on strike that day, and realize you're not. "*Bofff!*" you exclaim loudly, and the waiter looks at you like, "*Oui,* I understand. I also have to be at work today and that is—'ow you say—very *bofff.*"

You arrive at work, where you are greeted by your assistant/lover, Marguerite, who reminds you that today is the last day that you can decide if you would like to be transferred to the New York office. You consider it: New York. It's a great city. You'd be a great asset to the company, not to mention a gift to America. You'd be like the Statue of Liberty, but in Prada loafers, not those disgusting Chacos sandals she wears. Plus, the company is offering you a New York salary, which is more than you make in Paris. Like, WAY more. Mostly it's because the cost of living in New York is higher, but also, it's because it's America. And let's be real, it's also because you deserve it. I mean, you would have to go to a specialized French bakery to get a decent croissant over there. Their idea of a good pastry is a lukewarm croissant from Pret A Manger, which is basically just a 7-Eleven that studied abroad. For that reason alone, they should pay you some sort of worker's compensation. The company *is* offering you a $75,000 per year raise, which in Euros is something like 72 square centimeters.

To be able to go to New York, your office needs to file for an L-1 visa.

WHAT IS AN

L-1 VISA?

L-1 visas are awarded to temporary intracompany transferees in managerial or highly skilled positions. That's immigration talk for "No dumbs! No poors!"

L-1 visas are only issued when a multinational company requests one. So, mom-and-pop shops cannot request these unless they have an office in Germany where Mom and Pop Shop, Inc. is known as MommenVaderShoppen.

You can qualify for an L-1 visa if your company wants to open a US office for your business, but the company must be able to prove:

- They have a physical location for the new office;
- The employee has been an executive or manager for one continuous year in the three years before filing the petition; and
- The new office will support an executive or managerial position within one year of the approval of the petition. That means you have to keep the job for a year!
- They are willing to watch all episodes of *The Office* and admit that the British version is just not as good because Steve Carrell adds a level of heart that Ricky Gervais just doesn't have the range to play.

FILING FEES

Form I-129 USCIS L-1 visa filing fee: **$460**

Fraud prevention and detection fee: **$500**

DS-160 form MRV filing fee: **$190**

Premium Processing fee (optional): **$2,500**

Form I-539 L-2 visa filing fee for L-2 dependent change of status or extension: $370

Legal fees: **Vary**

IF YOU PROVIDE THE LAWYERS HIRED BY YOUR
MULTINATIONAL CORPORATION WITH THE DOCUMENTS
THEY NEED TO FILE YOUR VISA APPLICATION,

》 CONTINUE TO THE NEXT PAGE 》

IF YOU REFUSE TO PROVIDE THE LAWYERS HIRED BY YOUR
MULTINATIONAL CORPORATION WITH THE DOCUMENTS THEY
NEED BECAUSE YOU SAY, "MAIS 'OW ARE YEW SUPPOSED TO
KNOWWE OU EST YOUR BIRTH CERTIFICATE?"

■ TURN TO PAGE 20 ■

■

YOU PROVIDE THE LAWYERS HIRED BY YOUR MULTINATIONAL CORPORATION WITH THE DOCUMENTS THEY NEED TO FILE YOUR VISA APPLICATION.

After two weeks, you have successfully applied and received an L-1 visa! *Quelle bonne chance!*

The company also provided L-2 dependent visas for your wife, Annette, and your children, Camembert and Roquefort! But not one for your lover, Marguerite! This immigration system is terrible!

THE END

■

YOU REFUSE TO PROVIDE THE LAWYERS HIRED BY YOUR MULTINATIONAL CORPORATION WITH THE DOCUMENTS THEY NEED.

You look out the window of your office building in the La Defense neighborhood of Paris. From there you can see the Eiffel Tower, the hills of Montmartre, and the abomination that is the Tour Montparnasse. It haunts you to think how this black, imposing colossus destroyed the skyline of your beautiful city. Then you remember New York is full of skyscrapers. Just eyesore after eyesore after eyesore. Then you remember that in New York, you don't get all of August off to go to the mountains or the beach or to some sleepy town in the countryside where they've been making wine for the past seven hundred years and blaming all the problems of modern France on African immigrants for the past twelve to fifteen. New York doesn't have a patisserie on every corner, right next to a tobacco shop and a supermarket that sells cookies with racist cartoon mascots. And, worst of all, New York doesn't have a Disneyland. You might be forced to go to Legoland. Or worse: to Six Flags . . . in New Jersey.

"*Quelle horreur!*" you think to yourself. "I cannot live like this!" You call Marguerite into your office and tell her to remove the paperwork from your desk. You are staying in "gay Paree" and keeping your incredibly successful job.

That night at a brasserie in the 7th arrondissement, you go celebrate that you don't have to move to a place with unsophisticated Americans. You're joined by your wife, Annette, and your children, Camembert and Roquefort. And by your lover, Marguerite. *Quelle bonne chance!*

THE END

■

UPON SEEING YOUR REFLECTION,
YOU SEE AN ELEGANT WOMAN.

A sudden realization comes to you. Your name is Elise Marie Chocolatine de la Javert Valjean, and you're the heiress to the Bonne Maman jam fortune. Your *maman*, Mme Celine Marie Baguette de la Javert Valjean, is THE *bonne maman*. Your whole life, you've lived in utmost privilege. You grew up in Versailles; your first boyfriend was Babar, the king of the elephants; and you were educated at the Sorbonne, where you graduated magna cum laude in Looking Chic Sans Effort. However, you've spent your whole life in your mother's shadow. Her delicious, sweet, and sticky shadow. At every gala you attend, the question is always, "'ow is your *maman*? She is still *bonne, oui*?"* And you hate it. This house—this house you inherited from your mom—it is slowly crushing you and your spirit. It is the house that peach preserves built. And you must get out of here.

---

*The French dialogue in this section will be used irresponsibly and stereotypically. It is okay. They did so much colonizing. We can laugh at them.

You get dressed without a shower because you're French but also because you've decided your look is Olsen-twin chic, leaving your one-night stand, a soccer player who has perfect abs and a neck tattoo of his own face, and go to breakfast.

You leave your palace (it's more like one of those big, beaux arts–style manor houses, 'ow do you say . . . *un palais*?) and, in an act of rebelliousness, head to a seedy and unsafe neighborhood like Le Marais or Saint-Germain-des-Prés. It is so scary to be around people who only own one Mercedes-Benz. You decide to have breakfast (coffee, black; cigarettes, white with little orange bit) at an al fresco table at a cafe. The waiter sees you and says, "*Mon dieu, mademoiselle*, you are so beautiful, it is making me want to—*comment on dit*—run away with you and kill a policeman, like in that Jean-Luc Godard movie." You giggle. If you ran away with every Jean-Paul Belmondo out there who has told you they think you're so beautiful they want to run away with you and kill a policeman, like in that Jean-Luc Godard movie, you would be on the Interpol Most Wanted list for murdering policemen. The man says, "Let me bring you some food for free. A croissant? A baguette? A viennoise?" You settle on any pastry, since you know this is a real French establishment and they will bring you the secret French pastries that don't make you fat that they only serve to other French people. Then, *tragédie* strikes.

The waiter brings you a croissant with some of that French butter that doesn't give you a lactose stomachache, and a tiny jar of jam. It is Bonne Maman. Even here, in a place so far from your life of comfort, you can't escape the gloopy, fig-preserve-laden reach of your mom's grubby, little, confit-filled hands. You must do something. You must escape. You long for a place where you can be your own self. Where no one cares that your fortune is inherited, they only care that you have a fun, nonthreatening European accent. You realize you can never escape your legacy if you stay in Europe. You know you can't move to Asia because you can't speak any Asian languages. In fact, you only speak French and English, and what are you going to do? Move to England? As a French person, there is no greater dishonor. And you're not moving to Canada; they have the English Queen on their money BY CHOICE. So, you grab your phone and look up how a rich person can move to the United States. Suddenly, you get a phone call from someone you have not spoken to in years.

IF YOU IGNORE THE CALL AND REALIZE YOU NEED AN EB-5 IMMIGRANT INVESTOR VISA,

■　**TURN TO PAGE 28**　■

IF YOU TAKE THE CALL,

■　**TURN TO PAGE 32**　■

WHAT IS AN
EB-5 INVESTOR VISA?

The EB-5 Investor Program was established in 1990 to stimulate the US economy and create jobs. Like most ideas from the '90s, it's not terrible but it was probably thought of under the influence of monumental amounts of cocaine.

The program allows foreign investors who are proprietors or partners of a business enterprise to move to the US if they create ten full-time positions for employees in the United States. These jobs must go to legal US permanent residents. Which is hard, because the only people who want to work in America are immigrants, and they are not always documented.

You are also required to invest about $1,000,000 in your own capital to start this company and create these jobs. Unfortunately, this capital cannot be acquired by unlawful means, so you can't really start a data analytics company in Tupelo, Mississippi, if you got your money selling illegal whale organs on the dark web. However, there is no rule that says that you can't make your money in a pyramid scheme. I guess what I'm saying

here is, you can make a lot of money selling PlantLyfe supple-
ments. Please, I have so many boxes of them in my bathtub, but
trust me, these things practically sell themselves. How would
you like to be your own boss? Call me!

FILING FEES

Form I-526 Immigrant petition of a standalone investor: **$3,675**

Form I-485 (if adjustment of status is filed within the United States): **$1,140**

Form I-829 Petition for investor to remove conditions: **$3,750**

■

YOU IGNORE THE CALL AND REALIZE YOU NEED AN EB-5 IMMIGRANT INVESTOR VISA.

You realize that if you want to move to America, like all your friends who have done it before you (other rich people, like your friends the twins: Moët and Chandon), you need an investor visa. It won't be cheap. You realize you need to invest at least $1,000,000 in a large city like New York or Los Angeles or $500,000 in a smaller area that needs more jobs. Plus, you need to hire at least five or ten workers (depending on how much money you invest in the business) who are all legally allowed to work in the United States. It feels like a lot of trouble and a lot of money, and it is, but isn't it a small price to pay to finally feel like you've made something out of yourself? It isn't. It is a big price to pay to finally feel like you've made something out of yourself.

You move to Toledo, Ohio, because you visited Toledo, España when you were younger. Not that you're old. You're in your thirties, but you're French, so your metabolism is in your twenties, but your lungs are in your sixties. Toledo, Ohio, is not like you imagined. It is not a former capital of a once mighty caliphate, nor is it the home of kings, unless you count America's one true king: Burger. But of all the cities in Ohio, Toledo is undoubtedly the fourth most populous.

It is nice and still a city, and above all it is a good place to start a business. You purchase a space in downtown Toledo, and because you're missing the real, perfect, puffy pastries of your homeland, you choose to open your own bakery: Patisserie Mademoiselle. You can't really bake, but you can hire someone who can. You'd hire the baker who made you that pastry the day you decided to move to America, but unfortunately, you have to hire American workers for your visa. You decide to hold French baking auditions because at some point your life has become a Hallmark movie. This is, by far, the most exciting thing to happen in Toledo since 2010, when they shot an episode of *Supernatural* there.

The finalists are a young man named Mauricio and a woman named Keisha. Before their last challenge, you praise them and remind them that they are both amazing bakers who, had they been born in France, would be treated like movie stars. Then you clarify: "Yes, in France, patisserie bakers are stars. They have patisserie premieres and croissant-themed award shows, and there's a walk of fame in Lyon, but instead of stars it has eclairs." They seem even more confused. "Wouldn't that just be an oval?" says Mauricio. And you can't argue with that. Then you give them their last challenge: make a perfect *mille-feuille*, which is French for "one thousand sheets" because that's more poetic than saying, "like five or six layers of puff pastry filled with cream that you're going to scarf down, piggy." Not only is it very hard to make, it is also impossible to spell.

Mauricio and Keisha get to work, and after about three hours (oven quality depending), you are presented with two beautiful, soft, crispy, creamy mille-feuille. Two thousand *feuilles* of creamy perfection. You try them and know what you knew in your heart all along, that it is possible to love two bakers at once. You tell them the truth, that it is impossible for you to pick one of them, and they look you straight in the eye. Mauricio says, "Uh, so, is there a way you could hire both of us?" And you realize that you need to hire ten employees, so yeah, it's no problem. You ask them if they want to also be your lovers, but Keisha says she's married, and also not interested, no offense. Mauricio is into it.

Your patisserie opens and it's an immediate hit. A few months in, a young woman walks in and orders a croissant. She takes a bite and says it's the best croissant she's ever had. "Thank you," you say. "It's the secret French flour we use that makes everything sweet but not too sweet." The young woman tells you she is the daughter of the owner of a local supermarket chain and asks you if you'd let her sell the pastries at her dad's stores. You say, *"Mais bien sur!"* When she looks at you, confounded, you say, "That is French for 'fuck yes.'" She says she'll let her people call your people, to which you respond that you and your family no longer own any people. That was your great-grandmother in Martinique. She laughs, and as she walks out the door, you realize you never asked for her name. She turns and says, "Kroger. Gro Cerie Kroger, but my friends call me Grocery." You ask if that's German.

Two years later, you and Mauricio are married and have two beautiful mixed-race babies called Camembert and Cotija. You have settled into a sweet, suburban American life. You have almost forgotten your past in France. It's been so long since you've said *"putain"* or *"bof!"* or "non, non, we are not racists. Look at our diverse football team. They are the best of the French, unless they lose, in which case they are Congolese and Algerian." It's been even longer since you called your *maman*. She doesn't even know about your kids. Not that she's ever called you. She was always too busy crushing figs and oranges into sticky, sticky success. You remind yourself that you were able to leave the nest and you're doing incredibly well. Patisserie Mademoiselle is the most successful purveyor of baked goods for people who are running late to their book clubs. It's a booming market.

One day, you find yourself in the supermarket. Not the Kroger; the nice one owned by a tech company that doesn't sell detergent unless it's called something like Ralph's Organic Stain Detacher (because the word "remover" removes the stain's agency). It's where your pastries sell best. You find your packaged buns and rolls. Right next to them, a little table with a sign that reads: "Goes great with." Under the sign sit a half-dozen jars of jam. Not just any jam. The best jam. Your *bonne maman*'s jam. A young man carrying a baby in a papoose and holding a bag of croissants in his hand stops, then grabs a jar of jam. You smile. You think to yourself, perhaps I should call *maman*.

THE END

■

YOU TAKE THE CALL.

"*Allô?*" you say. Confused, maybe even flustered. This can't be him. He's an important person now. He can't just be calling your phone number. But then you hear his voice. His sweet, yet strong voice. A voice that tells you "I will be kind to you, I will fight for you, and I can wear the shit out of a suit." The voice of your ex-boyfriend, Babar, king of the elephants.

Babar wasn't always king of the elephants. When you first met him, you were both studying at the Lycée des Oligarques du Futur in the Swiss Alps. You, an heiress hoping to learn the subtle arts of having money and dining well. Him, a simple lad on a scholarship who barely had anything. No clothes other than the shirt on his back, mostly because he was an elephant standing on his hind legs. You two felt a connection immediately. He was sweet and curious and so unlike anyone you'd met before. All the other boys at the lycée seemed so . . . basic, and boring, and trunk-less. You taught him about the world. About how he had to use cutlery even if he didn't have opposable thumbs. You taught him that in the human world, people ride in cars and mopeds and hot air balloons. You taught him that green looks great on him. You got him a green snowsuit and he became the first elephant to ever ski. You loved your time in the mountains. It was up on those slopes where you and Babar shared your first kiss. He was your first love. Your first . . . well, a lady doesn't tell, does she?

You spent every hour of every day together. And your parents liked him. Sure, they were a little shocked. I mean, after all, he was not French. But they learned to love his genuine spirit. You both spoke of marriage. In the way young people do, with as much impatience as ignorance and infatuation. And then, one day, they arrived. His two cousins. You will never forget them: Arthur and Celeste. Celeste. There's a reason it rhymes with *déteste*. Celeste and Arthur took him from you. And soon after that, he became king. You read somewhere that some sort of council of elders voted him king because he knew so much about humans. And why did he know so much, you asked yourself? Who taught him? But no one could answer. No one would.

On the day of his coronation, you watched with your entire family on television. You were rich, so you had the cable TV package with the Elephant Nation TV channel. Your mother said, "You must be the only person in the world who allows an elephant to escape her grasp." Then she shoved more jam down her gullet. Your eyes filled with tears, but still, you could see him standing and waving next to Celeste. That cousin. That cousin he had married! Because a king needs a queen, my liege. No western king is a bachelor. Now, sure. Elephants are almost extinct, but surely there was one female elephant in the whole kingdom that wasn't related to him, right? You saw him wear a thick red cape, a sign of power in the west that surely he had been told to wear. But under the cape, under all the pomp and circumstance, you saw he was wearing a green suit. You never heard from him again. Until today.

You try to play it cool, but you could never play it cool with him. He admits he could never play it cool with you. He talks about how much he misses France. About the pressure of the throne. He tells you his country is becoming a true democracy now. He is abdicating. You can't believe what you're hearing.

"But your whole life! Your whole kingdom!"

"I can't keep the fantasy that kings are needed in the twenty-first century."

"Yes." You have to agree. "Or else you will become a tyrant. Or worse—English."

"It's time," he says. "Plus, I miss my days of skiing. I can't wait to go back. I even got myself a new snowsuit. Green, of course."

"Like you wore at your coronation," you say.

"Like you taught me to wear," he responds.

And any trace of resistance, any hint of intransigence evaporates from your body.

"I miss you, Elise."

"You've made your choice."

"That, I have."

He mentions that he got divorced. Amicable. When there was no need for a king, there was no need to keep the facade. They never loved each other, Celeste and him. But the pressure of the throne. The responsibility of a kingdom. They had to be together. Celeste actually was the one who suggested the divorce. She lives in America now, with a lovely guy named Mauricio. She's in movies. Producing, not *in* them.

You listen. You aren't sure what to think. He asks if he can see you. He will be in the Alps soon. He says he understands if you don't want to.

"But" he says. "I truly believe there is a world where we can be together again. Far from everything. Back in our mountains. I own some property there. We could get away. For a little bit."

You hang up after talking for a few more minutes. You pay your bill and get up. Your mother calls you. You ignore her calls as you walk into the Galeries Lafayette. You ignore her calls as you buy a new snowsuit and a large suitcase, the kind you buy when you intend to be gone for a long time. You're gonna go marry a fucking elephant.

THE END

HARD

Your adventure begins as most adventures do: you're a young person longing for a quest! Usually a man, but sometimes a woman and/or person of color, especially in modern retellings and more recent movies. You live a pleasant and comfortable life, but you long for something more. Something else. You know there's a whole world out there with opportunities and new experiences. You know there's a special place for you out there. A magical place with things called "Greek life," "red Solo cups," and "grade curves." That magical place is a US college. Before you start your quest, you must ask yourself a very important question: "Do you like The Smiths?"

"WHO ARE THE SMITHS?"

◆ **TURN TO PAGE 38** ◆

"WELL, YEAH, I KNOW WHO MORRISSEY IS."

◆ **TURN TO PAGE 86** ◆

◆

"WHO ARE THE SMITHS?"

Yes, who are The Smiths, indeed? You have no time for the melodramatic crooning of a weird English guy who will later turn out to be a Brexit voter.*

Quick question, are you a model? A modern Apollo/Aphrodite?

IF YOU ARE A DEMIGOD AMONG MERE MORTALS,

◆ **TURN TO PAGE 162** ◆

IF YOU ARE NOT A MODEL,

◆ **CONTINUE TO THE NEXT PAGE** ◆

Hi, Kevin here. We don't really know that Morrissey voted for Brexit for sure, but he was in the papers saying it was great. Normally that would be enough, but British newspapers will print anything.

◆

YOU ARE NOT A MODEL.

You're a STEM major. You're all busy making robots, discovering the intricacies of microbiomes in the Amazon, solving an equation that has befuddled the greatest minds of four generations, or, in the case of the economics majors, trying to come up with a way to make capitalism make sense. Keep going, chaps. We believe in you!

In this particular case, your name is Camila Martínez. You're the daughter of Fabrizio and Carla and you live in a lovely house in Buenos Aires. In your short life, you've seen how precarious life can get even for the supposed middle class. Also, you love nature, a trait you inherited from your dad. He is a hiker, and he climbs mountains instead of going to therapy. It's both healthy and unhealthy. In your time in college, you realize you want to work in renewable energy programs. You chalk that up to your love for nature and for not having to spend your seventies learning how to make armor out of barbed wire and beef jerky to fight in the Water Wars that are definitely coming. Also, while you recognize it is a gaudy, excessive, opulent, and reckless monument to a single company owned by an accused antisemite, you had a pretty great time at Walt Disney

World when you went there as a kid. Sure, you were ten, but even as you've aged, you know it's pretty magical. I mean come on, the moment a little girl sees Cinderella's castle for the first time? Top ten things to ever witness. So, you think it would be a shame if The Magic Kingdom were to become the world's first underwater park.*

"I mean, how would it even work? You can't be Space Mountain if you are also Sea Mountain. This is basic stuff, people!" you yell during an *asado*† at your uncle's house.

Your entire family stares at you, puzzled, but appreciative of your passion. Then in comes your one cousin. You know the one. The one who keeps trying to pitch your dad on his new venture. This time: crypto for dogs. It's all powered by quantum computing, AI, and the laptop his buddy Fabio is running in his garage. He looks at you and says, "But what if climate change isn't real?" To which you respond with the obvious answer: "If climate change isn't real, we get new, cool ways to make energy better and cheaper for everyone in the world and depend less on oil and oil states, simultaneously giving countries in the global south a chance to become energy leaders. Also, if it's real, penguins lose their homes. Is that what you want, Javier? Homeless penguins? Look at him," you say to your entire family, as you point at him. "He wants to make penguins homeless!"

Your family shuns your cousin forever because the image of a little penguin holding a bindle and asking for money outside of a

---

Hey, Kevin here again. Um. Yeah, please don't sue us, Disney. I am terrified of your lawyers. Half of them were my bullies at NYU law school. Yes, there are bullies in law school. They steal your lunch money and make fun of your appellate briefs.

† That's Spanish for "barbecue." It's important for English-language readers in the US to learn Spanish words because, statistically, that's gonna be the language of the people your kids or grandkids are gonna marry.

Starbucks is just too sad. He is disowned by your *abuelita* and kicked out of the *asado*. Your family is all on your side. They understand the importance of renewable energies, but they're not gonna stop eating meat. And neither are you. You're from Argentina, after all.

Your uncle asks where the best places to continue your studies are, and you tell him that there are two countries in the west that are actually investing time and money into renewable energy research: Germany and the United States. Do you speak German?

"JA! NATÜRLICH!"

◆   **TURN TO PAGE 42**   ◆

"NOPE. I DON'T SPEAK GERMAN."

◆   **TURN TO PAGE 43**   ◆

◆

"*JA! NATÜRLICH!*" YOU USE THE MONEY YOU DO NOT HAVE AND LEARN GERMAN.

*Du sprichst Deutsch! Fantastisch! Du zählst null Euro für dein Doktoratstudium und heiratest die Liebe deines Lebens. Auf Wiedersehen!**

DAS ENDE

---

*"Yes, of course! You speak German! Wonderful. You spend zero euros in your doctoral studies and marry the love of your life. Goodbye!"

◆

"NOPE. I DON'T SPEAK GERMAN."

You choose to go to the University of East Dakota. Since it is a public university, it is slightly cheaper than other options in the US, with tuition and board costing about $45,000 a year. Since you are a STEM major, you can do mental math to find out how much that is in your local currency: twentyleven-thousand sevenhumber-and-flourty bajillion Celsiusbucks. You fill out the application forms for the school and you reach a question you've been expecting:

Will you require financial aid?

IF YOU REQUIRE FINANCIAL AID,

◆ TURN TO PAGE 44 ◆

IF YOU MAGICALLY FOUND $50,000 IN YOUR POCKETS
AND DO NOT REQUIRE FINANCIAL AID ANYMORE,

◆ TURN TO PAGE 91 ◆

◆

YOU REQUIRE FINANCIAL AID.

Great. There is none. Most American universities do not provide financial aid for international students unless you are pursuing a PhD. And even in those cases, they offer meager stipends for students who are not allowed to work anywhere except for the university. Try going to school at Florida International University and living in Miami with a $1,000/month stipend.

AUTHOR'S NOTE: Please don't try to do this. You will die. Also, you can't try going to school in Florida, as school there will soon be illegal.

"*JA! NATÜRLICH!*" TO USE THE MONEY YOU DO NOT HAVE AND LEARN GERMAN,

◆ **TURN TO PAGE 42** ◆

TO APPLY FOR FINANCIAL AID IN YOUR OWN COUNTRY AND MOVE TO AMERICA,

◆ **CONTINUE TO THE NEXT PAGE** ◆

◆

YOU APPLY FOR FINANCIAL AID IN YOUR OWN COUNTRY AND MOVE TO AMERICA.

You've decided to embark on the exhausting journey of applying for financial aid to be able to study. It's the perfect decision for anyone who saw the immigration process and said, "You know what I need? More paperwork."

You begin by looking up the biggest, most prestigious scholarships. You know, the ones named after white guys who were actually super racist, like segregationist senator J. William Fulbright; virulent white supremacist Cecil Rhodes; and the most hateful of them all, Eustace B. AthleticMerit. You realize that many of these aren't designed for you to study in the United States, and that many more are only useful for your postgraduate studies. You look into other forms of financial aid. Your country offers local loans with crazy-high interest rates that may be forgiven on the promise of returning to your country to teach what you have learned. Turns out it's not those who can't do who teach. It's those who can't afford to pay a 9 percent per annum interest rate. It's borderline extortionate. It's criminal. Which gives you an idea. You could . . . just find financial aid from . . . less legal means. After all, America loves a criminal—just look at Al Capone, Billy the Kid, and whoever invented oatmeal raisin cookies.

IF YOU PROCURE YOUR FINANCIAL AID LEGALLY,

◆   **CONTINUE TO THE NEXT PAGE**   ◆

IF YOU PROCURE YOUR FINANCIAL AID LESS THAN LEGALLY,

◆   **TURN TO PAGE 82**   ◆

◆

YOU PROCURE YOUR FINANCIAL AID LEGALLY.

Alright, so you're going to school in America, but you're definitely going to be in a lot of debt. That means one thing and one thing only: once you graduate, you're gonna need a job, pronto. That's Spanish for "pronto," which of course is Italian for "pronto," which, of course, is Portuguese for "ON TIME, NOT QUICKLY." To be able to address your college debt, you start applying for as many jobs as you can, and in every single job application you are met with that little accursed question that breaks your heart every time you see it. It's almost cruel how it's usually the last question in every online job application. It comes after you've input your education and your higher-than-your-US-born-classmate's GPA. After you've input all your work experience. After you've written a cover letter that explains that it is your dream to work for INSERT COMPANY NAME DON'T MESS UP AND FORGET TO CHANGE IT LIKE YOU DID IN THE LAST JOB APPLICATION WHY ON EARTH DOES EVERY COMPANY ASK FOR A COVER LETTER? NO ONE EVER READS THESE. It's right next to one of those stupid little clickable boxes. It reads, tauntingly:

Will you now or in the future require sponsorship to work in the United States?

Now or in the future? How are you supposed to know? The future is unknowable. In the future, you might be the CEO of McGoogleBuxAppleheiser-Busch, the last American company that owns everything; or you could be one of the mercenaries who protect the underground bunker of King Jeff of House Bezos from the raiders and the mutant capybaras who are finally punishing humankind for what we did to the planet; or you can marry an American and never need any kind of sponsorship. All of these scenarios are equally as likely, so it is impossible to answer that question honestly. But that's just the beginning of your problems with that question. Because above all, it's also the confirmation of something you had started to suspect in your years of study in the US but that you didn't really want to admit. A secret they don't tell you in visa interviews and in college brochures. A secret that International Student Offices in colleges all across America choose to believe isn't real: the secret that your grades don't really matter that much. Normally, that is a good thing you say to a student. Because it really, really does not matter what grade you get in your "The Semiotics of *Seinfeld*" class, but in the case of immigrants it's a reminder that your grades, and by extension your excellence, is not even the bare minimum. It is unimportant. In true American fashion, the ability for you to remain here is determined by your job. And jobs are provided by companies. And companies tend to know one thing about immigration: it's a fucking hassle. The truth is that immigrants aren't taking good jobs from Americans. Americans are taking jobs from immigrants with higher GPAs and work ethics than Americans.

For you to successfully stay in the United States, you will need to get a job that will sponsor you in the future. That doesn't mean that if you work at State Farm, you have to walk around wearing a State Farm logo, like a human NASCAR car.* What it does mean is that State Farm or whichever company likes you so much that they choose to blow a sizable amount of money to sponsor you has to tell the government that they REALLY, REALLY like you. Not like, just *like* you. Like, they *like-like* you. That means they ask the government to issue you a work visa, which is an incredibly expensive and time-consuming process because, you guessed it, it's an immigration process. But that's a problem for the future, because thankfully, for now, you have OPT.

---

*Do they call them NASCAR cars? Or just NASCARS? Feels like NASCARS is a better name. Call Mr. NASCAR and pitch this million-dollar idea to him.

WHAT IS

OPT?

OPT stands for Optional Practice Training. It can also stand for Outpatient Physical Therapy, Off-Post Training, and Ouch! Penis Trap! But, for the purposes of this book, it means Optional Practice Training.

OPT is a temporary employment that is available to F-1 student visa holders, directly related to their course of study. You can only apply for OPT if you are in school and only get it for the work you will do *after* school. That means you can only get a barista job right out of college if you have a Bachelor of Science in Espressonomy from the University of North Caramel-latte at Chapel Hill. Immigrants, you don't get survival jobs. What do you even need those for? To survive?

To apply for OPT, your school must recommend you for it. Most international student offices will do it, but imagine if there's someone at your school's ISO who doesn't vibe with you. Just in case, be nice to Derek at the front desk. He's going through a bad breakup. After your school has recommended you, you can send the government your application, along with $410 payable only by check or money order. Since you're a baby college student, let this book explain what those are: A check is like Venmo but on paper, but it's not cash. It's better than cash because instead of old presidents, they can have Tom and Jerry on them. No one knows what a money order is.

If you opt (pronounce like a word) to take OPT (do not pronounce like a word), the government will issue you an Employment Authorization Card, which will allow you to work and remain in the US for one (1) year. The government will not issue you a spectral, pale, menacing man in a long, dark robe who holds an hourglass to signify the unending passage of time and who you can see in the corner of your eye at every moment, even when you sleep. That guy is only in your mind. Hopefully.

NOTE: STEM students can apply for a two-year extension on their OPT. Art students, you already have it easy enough. Stop whining and make me that iced brown sugar oat milk shaken espresso.

FILING FEE

$410

IF YOU HAVE OPT AND YOU'RE A STEM STUDENT,

◆   TURN TO PAGE 54   ◆

IF YOU HAVE OPT AND YOU'RE NOT A STEM STUDENT,

◆   TURN TO PAGE 109   ◆

♦

YOU HAVE OPT AND YOU'RE A STEM STUDENT.

OPT is very nice, but it's not something you can explain in an Indeed .com job application. Because the question is not "Do you need sponsorship?" It's "Will you now or in the future require sponsorship?" And once you click yes on that box, you might self-screen yourself out of a lot of jobs. That's why, at the end of your studies, you'll only have two job offers: one from a small, third-party energy provider based in St. Louis where you could really make a difference, and one from a company that for legal reasons we will only refer to as "The Electric Car Company," which, come on, that's super cool! You will need sponsorship to work for both companies, but you agree with both hiring managers that you can deal with that in the future. Sure, kicking that can down the road may result in some companies exploiting you by making you do more work than others, but companies would never do that, right? Also, if you deal with it in the future, maybe the Jetsons* will be there.

---

*During the process of writing this book, my editor very fairly pointed out that young people might not know who the Jetsons are, which made me feel

TO TAKE THE JOB AT THE SMALL COMPANY IN ST. LOUIS,

◆   **TURN TO PAGE 56**   ◆

TO TAKE THE JOB AT THE ELECTRIC CAR COMPANY,

◆   **TURN TO PAGE 77**   ◆

incredibly old. That said, it's perfectly reasonable for people not to know about a TV show that hasn't aired in decades. The Jetsons are a cartoon family in an animated sitcom by the same name created in 1962 by Hanna-Barbera Productions; it's basically *The Flintstones* but in "the future." While they do have a robot maid and flying cars, they got many other futuristic things wrong—except they do talk to their bosses via a TV screen, so in a way they predicted Microsoft Teams. If you are a person who didn't know who the Jetsons are, now you do. If you are a person who wants to let us know that you DID know who the Jetsons are, please send a letter to 98 East Pfefferport Road, Brownsfield Junction, Vermont 05471-02938.

That's not my address. Nor my editor's. It's actually the address of the Vermont Service Center of the USCIS, but I think it would be funny if they got random letters that said, "I know who the Jetsons are."

Kevin here! This is absolutely not the USCIS's address. And please do not mail anyone ANYTHING.

◆

YOU TAKE THE JOB AT THE SMALL COMPANY IN ST. LOUIS.

You have moved to St. Louis. Of all the cities in Missouri, it is certainly the second largest. St. Louis was originally founded by the French, which explains its name, its obsession with a tall, metal landmark, and the way its police department treats Black people. You enjoy the city for what it is: a midsized American city just like most other midsized American cities, designed for cars, but with some really special things happening in the newly renovated downtown. Half of the buildings in there used to be factories but now they're tattoo parlors, microbreweries, and, once a month, every storefront becomes an art gallery where people play Dungeons & Dragons, and also there's axe throwing or some white bullshit like that. Also, everything is lit by Christmas lights inside Mason jars (no exceptions).

For almost three years, you've worked for Capacitor Energy. It's a clean energy startup that doesn't sound like it's about clean energy. See, you live in a red state, and implying that climate change is real is bad for business, but telling people they can save money if they get their energy from solar or wind is good for business. Your bosses are an idealistic young man named Curtis Hines III and his father, Curtis Sr., who you assume is Curtis Hines II, but he just goes by Sr., so that means there must be a Curtis Sr. Sr. who is the original Curtis Hines, but you've never met him. Curtis is pretty cool; he invites you to Thanksgiving every year, and you've built a relationship with his family. You're Aunt Camila to his two daughters, Kayleighn and Ashelaine. One Christmas, you couldn't travel home to Argentina, so you spent the day with them, helping them build Legos and learning how to politely say, "Wow, eggnog is fricking disgusting." You assume, but also you know, that Curtis wants to help you get your work visa so you can stay in the country.

However, his dad—who doesn't own the company, but who loaned Curtis a lot of money to get the business started—is a libertarian. He will be the first hurdle you need to clear. You ask Curtis if he could bring it up with his dad, and he agrees to do so. A couple of days later, Curtis tells you he wants to go to dinner with you and his dad, and that he's made a reservation at a restaurant that will hopefully make you feel at home. That restaurant is Chili's. You have so many questions, like "Do you know I'm from Argentina, not Mexico?" and "Isn't Chili's more Tex-Mex than Mexican?" and "Is this racist or just a joke?" But perhaps most importantly: "Does Chili's take reservations?"

You get there early. Thirty minutes before the time you'd agreed to meet. You're nervous. You've never met Curtis Sr. You wonder what he looks like. Even though you know he will just kind of look like Curtis, but older, you can't help but wonder if he looks like some sort of evil dad figure, like Darth Vader or Thanos or Mrs. Doubtfire (gaslighting your children and ex-wife into thinking you're a British woman is wrong. Also, those scratchy-looking '90s sweaters with cuckoo rhombus patterns are a crime.). You wonder if he's ever even heard of you before this. You start to panic. Why have you never met him at Thanksgiving? Or Christmas? Or the girls' birthday parties? Is it because he not-so-secretly hates immigrants? "Oh, god," you think, as you start anxiously shoveling complimentary chips and salsa into your mouth. "You're so screwed. This was such a dumb idea. You should've taken that job at The Electric Car Company. You know they have international workers. But then you'd have to work for That ONE Billionaire and that may not be worth it. This is so dumb." They walk in as you scarf the last chip from the little basket in your mouth. Curtis Sr. just kinda looks like a normal guy in his fifties. He's like Curtis if he had to work a little harder in life. He gives you the impression that he's had to do work that involves digging or cutting wood planks in a way that Curtis's tender little hands have never experienced. Curtis Sr. went to military school. Curtis Jr. went to an academy "with its own pedagogical approach to creativity." They come to greet you. Curtis gives you a hug and so does Curtis Sr.

"I've heard so much about you!" he exclaims. Here's the thing: Curtis Sr. is a complicated guy. Sure, he's a libertarian business owner, but he's also a nice Midwesterner from Missouri. He likes his money and the fact that he worked hard for it. That means he really appreciates how hard you've worked to get where you are. "I know a hard worker when I see one," he says. "And I know all the hard work you put in for my—sorry, Curtis's company." Turns out the reason you never saw him is because he has to spend the holidays with his second wife's family, and because he has an underground bunker where he's preparing for the end of the world, so he has to keep renovating it, and that's why he hasn't been able to go to the girls' birthdays recently. "But I always send a gift!" he adds. He's complicated. He hates the bureaucracy around your visa but loves that you're a cheap hire more than he hates the government. And you *are* a cheap hire, since companies must spend money to sponsor immigrants, on average companies pay immigrants less than they would pay citizens and residents for doing the same job. Not enough for it to be super egregious, but enough to make you go, "Wait, you pay Brendan WHAT?" It's an unfair labor practice, similar to one known as "how they treat women." They let you know they have agreed to sponsor your visa. "We'll go over the details later," says Curtis. "For now. We eat like *reyes.* That's kings, right?" You nod. You also burst into tears of joy, and you regret your meal choice as your happy tears hit the pan on your Mix & Match Sizzling Fajitas.

A month before your visa application and registration are due, you set up a meeting on their Google Calendar to explain why they have to decide if they will sponsor you soon. They told you to put it on their Google calendars, and you do. Except that in doing so, you access Curtis Sr.'s calendar and notice he has a recurring meeting labeled "SEXYTIMES" on Tuesdays at 8 p.m. The only other guest invited to that meeting is his new wife. She hasn't RSVP'd yet. You didn't need to know that about him, but now you do. This will in no way influence your story or your path in any way other than now possessing the knowledge that Curtis Sr. schedules sex. You will never bring it up with him or his son. You will never bring it up with his wife if she ever comes visit the office. But you will know. Every time you see all of them, you will have this knowledge. It's now seared into your brain. Not in a judging way. It's just there. Forever. You schedule your meeting and try to console yourself with the thought that at least when you're thinking about that meeting in Curtis Sr.'s calendar, you're not thinking about how you need an H-1B Work Visa.

WHAT IS AN
H-1B WORK VISA?

The H-1B work visa allows a company to hire workers in what the USCIS calls "specialty occupations." That just means you need a college degree, but mostly in the careers that give you desk jobs. Sorry, professional chefs, your house specialty doesn't count. Plus, spatchcocking is easy. The visa lasts for a period of up to three years, and it can be extended, but it can't last longer than six years. So, the maximum amount of time you can be on this visa is one senator's term, or about half the wait between *Avatar* movies.

To apply, you need to register online on a government website, present proof of your degree (so don't try to apply with an Olive Garden kids menu where you spelled out Harverd. Yes, Harverd), and file a Labor Certification Application (LCA), which is a scary immigration document, but at least it rhymes. The LCA has to certify that the employer will pay the immigrant a wage that is no less than the wage paid to similarly qualified workers; that they will provide working conditions that won't adversely affect other workers; and that there isn't a strike or work stoppage happening when the LCA was requested. Basically, it's a big document that says: "We're not like other employers, we're a cool employer."

What other documents must you file? Well, on the government's website, there is a list that includes eight forms, a letter from your employer, a letter from your attorneys, an item called "Addendums," and another item called "Other supporting documentation." It's so many documents, they have to have TWO items called "others."

Once your employer has registered you with the government, filed your LCA, and paid money to prove they really-really-really want to hire you, don't you get your visa? No, you don't. Why would they make this easy when they can make it dystopian? Welcome to the world of the H-1B Lottery.

The H-1B Lottery

Everything you need to know about the US Immigration Citizen and Immigration System is that they read Shirley Jackson and said, "Why don't we do *that*?" For reasons—*cough* racism *cough*—that make no sense, politicians who complain that "nobody wants to work no more" decided that we need a cap for work visas. The government will grant 65,000 new visas each year, with an additional 20,000 applications for those who have a master's degree or higher. Sounds pretty good, right? Wrong. It's actually really hard to get this because, according to the USCIS, in 2021, they received 274,237 applications. In 2022, it was 308,613. In 2023, it was 483,927. In 2024, it was 780,884. So, you do the math. No, seriously, you do the math. I don't want to do it. I want a drink.

If, and only if, you are selected in the lottery, your employer can send all your documents to the government on the first day of H-1B season: the worst season after the last season of *Game of Thrones*. The first day of H-1B season is April 1. That is not a joke. That is the real date. April Fool's Day is the day you must apply for your visa. It's not a prank, but it is a cruel, cruel joke.

NOTE: There are two other types of H-1B visas also subject to the lottery: the H-1B2, which is granted to Department of Defense "Cooperative Researchers," and the H-1B3, which is for models on short-term gigs. So, to get these, you need to be James Bond or Heidi Klum. And you still need to enter the lottery because this whole process is like some 2010s young adult dystopian novel called *The Maze of Hunger Power: Book 1.*

FILING FEES

$1,385

Registration Fee: **$10**

Fraud Prevention Fee: **$500**

Knowing That Your Entire Future Depends on a
Literal Lottery: **Your sanity**

After it takes you three hours to explain all of this to your employers, they ask you to explain it again. You do so, and they agree to try and get you an H-1B visa. You gather all the paperwork and register with the government. You must now wait for the lottery. You send your application on the day registration opens. You don't have to send it on that day, but since your chances to win the lottery are less than ten percent, you all assume it's better if you send it in sooner. Maybe the lottery rewards promptness. You can't really ascribe human feelings to the lottery, because if you do, it means that the lottery can be rigged, and if the lottery is rigged, then why would it be rigged in favor of you, a worker at a small company in St. Louis, over workers for companies who literally spend millions of dollars to lobby the government in favor of skilled immigration, like Meta, or Google, or the Keebler Elves? Oh, you think the Keebler Elves hire American elves? Sure, some of them are from Michigan or Nebraska, but they hire all sorts of English pixies, Spanish *duendes*, Irish leprechauns, Colombian *tunjos*, and Icelandic Yule Lads. They all work for the company and live in that one tree that is also a factory. The government really needs to investigate what's going on in there. So, you try not to think about the lottery as something corruptible. It is literally better to leave your entire life to chance.

And then it comes around: April 1, officially the beginning of the next business quarter. Unofficially, the cruelest prank that could exist. Oh, wait, no. That's not the cruelest prank. The cruelest prank is that you can't really find out if you won the lottery. The company's lawyer finds out. And then they call the company. And then the company tells you. This is some messed up Franz Kafka stuff. Seriously, it's about as vile, senseless, and haunting as awakening one morning from uneasy dreams to find yourself transformed in your bed into a gigantic insect.

You're supposed to go to the office like it's a normal day. So, you do. Because for everyone out there, it is. Because even though there are over 750,000 people like you out there applying for the same thing, no one around you seems to be having the same problem. One or two kids from your school, but you didn't really keep in touch with them because they were bio-chem engineering students who got really into that podcast where one guy is "just asking questions," but the questions are always things like "Why are trans people allowed to exist?" and never things like "Is my obsession with eating raw meat the reason my wife took the kids?" So, you sit on your work computer and try to pretend it's all okay, erratically opening and closing that weird Pinball game that came with old Windows XP computers. Yeah, your work computer still runs on Windows XP. Look, it's a small company in St. Louis, they're not made of money.

Then, you get an email from Curtis asking to please come to his office. You open the door. Curtis is there, as is Curtis Sr., and his new wife, who introduces herself as Bonnie. She is surprisingly age appropriate. You reprimand yourself for thinking Curtis Sr. would be kind of a perv, and realize he's never been one to you or to anyone you know. She notices. "You probably thought I'd be some spry little yoga teacher who fell for Curtis's wallet and stock options," she says. Curtis interjects, saying he doesn't believe in stocks and that most of his money is in cash and precious metals. You nod. Turns out they met at a gala. He went alone, and she went with a date who was more of a friend. They had a wonderful night together where they danced to Steely Dan, Sonny and Cher, John Prine, and other bands you have never heard of. "He knocked me off my feet with his sense of humor," she says. "And I fell for her knockers," he says, making her laugh. This all happened enough years after Curtis Sr. and Curtis's mom, Jenna, divorced in a non-acrimonious way. After a year of dating, they got engaged, and six months later they married at her church. They honeymooned in Florence. "It's not easy to find love when you're older," says Bonnie. "We're very lucky." It's a lovely story that you wish you could appreciate if it weren't for the fact that you know they're about to tell you if you won the lottery. Not the real one. The REAL one. The one with real consequences if you lose.

Curtis looks at you and says, "We got a call from the lawyer." Your feet are light. You feel like you are floating. You can hear nothing but the pounding of your heart, which obviously is bulging out of your chest like that little guy in *Alien*.

IF YOU ARE AS LUCKY AS BONNIE AND CURTIS SR.,

◆   **CONTINUE TO THE NEXT PAGE**   ◆

IF YOU ARE NOT AS LUCKY AS BONNIE AND CURTIS SR.,

◆   **TURN TO PAGE 70**   ◆

◆

YOU ARE AS LUCKY AS BONNIE AND CURTIS SR.

Hey, look at you! You're not one in a million, but you're certifiably one in about 780,000. You still kinda feel like you might throw up but it's good nausea. Not the kind you were feeling a few seconds ago. The kind you get when you go on a date and realize you just went on a date with the love of your life, or when you're seven and had too much cotton candy at the carnival and somehow, even though you're just seven, you know life doesn't get much better than having too much cotton candy at the carnival.

The Curtises cheer and pull out a cookie cake from behind Curtis's desk. On it, you see a little frosted American flag along with a message that reads, "You did it!" Which makes you wonder if they had another cookie cake in case they got the wrong call. One that read, "You didn't do it!" You smile, but you know the cookie cake is lying. On several levels. First, because all cookie cakes are lying because they're not cake, they're just a big cookie, and they should just be called "Large Cookie." Second, because you feel like you didn't really do anything. You did your best, but this was not your call. And there was nothing your talent or hard work could do to affect the outcome of this decision. The good nausea is quickly replaced with "what now" nausea. Because you're proud of what you've achieved, but also, it's kinda bullshit that you had to do all this. Not to mention . . . your destiny was decided by cosmic chance. Or divine intervention. Some people say God doesn't play dice, but right now, you can't help but feel God is hanging out with Loki, Coyote, the trickster god, and Cthulhu, playing Monopoly, and you're the little race car. Nothing was in your control, but nothing ever felt like anyone was in control at all. You know you should feel happy, but you can't help but feel that, in the end, chaos reigns. That's hardly the kind of message you want to put on a cookie cake. Nor would it fit.

You take a slice of cookie cake and return to your desk. You let out a big sigh and close your eyes. "This is a good thing." You pull out your phone to FaceTime your parents. They're having an *asado*. You forgot it was a holiday in your country today. It's not a holiday in this country. Which is now yours. You live here now. You have your family back home. And you have also found a family here. While you feel like you've reached the end of the colossal odyssey that is getting your visa, you realize that your adventure is just starting. And that now you are different. You are a being of two lands. A creature of two nations. You tell your parents. They are so happy for you. They don't have cookie cake, but they toast to you with Quilmes beer and glasses of red wine. You will see them soon, when you go get your visa stamped on your passport. They pass the phone around to the entire family so everyone can say congratulations. So everyone can wish you the best. So everyone knows you made it. You achieved your dreams. They pass the phone to *that* cousin. You know. The one who was being a jerk. The one who made fun of you for wanting to follow your dreams in what was only seven years ago but feels like a different lifetime ago. He says he's proud of you. You thank him and everyone else, and tell everyone you have to go. You have work to do.

THE END

♦

YOU ARE NOT AS LUCKY AS BONNIE AND CURTIS SR.

Wanna learn German now?

"*JA! NATÜRLICH!*" TO USE THE MONEY YOU DO NOT HAVE AND LEARN GERMAN,

♦ **TURN TO PAGE 42** ♦

"*NEIN!*"

♦ **CONTINUE TO THE NEXT PAGE** ♦

◆

Okay. Your options aren't looking great right now. In terms of staying in the United States legally. You could attempt to overstay your visa, a huge decision that will make it harder for you to find work, especially in a specialized field like yours, or you could return to your country to try and use what you learned in the United States. Or you could follow the strange woman in a magician's hat who's waiting for you in the office parking lot.

"Hurry!" she exclaims. "We must go. There are so many people waiting for you!"

You hesitate. Who is this woman with thin red strands of hair and a skintight pair of leather pants? Does she smell like piss or like cotton candy? Your nose can't decide.

"Well, what are you waiting for?" she asks.

You hesitate.

"You are the heir to the most powerful Magicks, no?"

You hesitate.

"You do believe in Magicks, right?"

IF YOU BELIEVE IN MAGICKS,

◆   CONTINUE TO THE NEXT PAGE   ◆

IF YOU DO NOT BELIEVE IN MAGICKS,

◆   TURN TO PAGE 76   ◆

◆

YOU BELIEVE IN MAGICKS.

You take the strange woman's hand and dash through a magical portal that opens behind her. In a second you realize you're not in Kansas anymore. You were never in Kansas in the first place, because St. Louis is in Missouri. But now you're in a meadow full of beautiful centaurs with the bodies of horses and the torsos and faces of Oscar Isaac and Gregory Peck and Usher. They are SO hot, but in a tender, loving way. They take one look at you and say, "She has arrived." You marry all of them so they can continue their species. They are generous lovers who always make sure you come first. Also, their penises are human penises and just the right length and girth. They're not horse penises. And the best part, since it's *their* species that needs to be continued, is that you don't get pregnant—they do. You live for five hundred years and become the matriarch of this society of horsemen lovers. Not all the times are easy. Sometimes you have to do the dishes (but only once every seven days), and there was that one time when those random teenagers ambushed you in the meadow. You were so scared. They wouldn't shut up about their super cool friend who is a lion but also Jesus. Thankfully, your husbands found you and took you to safety in your throne room, where you fell asleep on your throne/recliner made of clouds. You're pretty sure they trampled the teens. So, either they were wrong about their lion Jesus friend, or he was busy being everywhere and knowing everything.

One day, after a long day of sexy horseman boning, one of your progenies, a young horseling named Thaddeus, approaches you. He must be one of the newer foals. You can see the curiosity in his gaze. He bows and asks you, "Dearest queen of everything, giver of life, woman whose pores are always clear just because." You nod to him, allowing him to speak to you. "Where do you come from? You are not a horseman like us, but you are also not a horsewoman like our sisters." You realize he is one of the smart ones. You tell the tale of where you came from. A distant land called Argentina. The land of the Silver Lake. You longingly talk of soccer, and tango, and being the country with the most people who go to therapy per capita. Thaddeus listens intently, then ventures another question: "May I be bold, Queen Mother?" You allow him to. "If this place is as wondrous as you say, why leave?" And for a moment you remember the United States. A place you had fled to. A place you had long forgotten. You think of your time there and remember how it allowed a lousy lottery to decide your fate. Man, that was some bullshit. But then you realize that had you not been there, you would not have met the magical woman and that without her, you would've never ended up here. She lives here too! She has her own sexy horsemen tribe, and it's not territorial or anything. You guys hang out and have lunch every Wednesday in between horseman-macking sessions. You always make sure to thank her. After all, she's the reason you're surrounded by beautiful horsemen who look like Diego Luna. So, in your infinite wisdom, you look at Thaddeus and say, "Because I was destined to be here and not there." Thaddeus seems satisfied, and he trots away to learn algebra or some shit like that. Turns out centaurs love algebra and graphs, but in a hot way and not in a "let me explain to you the Excel spreadsheet I use for my fantasy football draft" kind of way. This day is the last time you ever think of America.

THE END

♦

YOU DO NOT BELIEVE IN MAGICKS.

You try to tell the woman you don't have any change, but before you can say anything, she's already put the rag over your nose and mouth. You come to in a bathtub in a room that would make the torture chambers in the movie *Saw* seem hygienic. You cough, and even though you're not a doctor, you know something's messed up in your lower back. You touch your side and feel the scar. You definitely have one fewer kidney than you used to. The door behind you opens, and the woman comes in. Oh yeah, she absolutely smells like piss. She cackles. You ask her to let you go. She cackles again. "No," she says. "You're gonna stay here until you teach me how to change my Apple ID password. All my children moved out, and I don't remember my old password." You realize you'll be trapped here until the day you die.

THE END

◆

YOU TAKE THE JOB AT THE ELECTRIC CAR COMPANY.

This is the sensible choice. You're moving to one of the top companies in the United States to work with a multinational team on a product that helps the environment, and your boss is a genius immigrant. What could go wrong?

This is not a rhetorical question. The thing that goes wrong is that the Billionaire* who owns The Electric Car Company is dumped by his girlfriend and his adult child disowns him, so he becomes a far-right, radicalized monster. You get transferred from The Electric Car Company to his brand-new company, B0nr, the everything messaging, banking, crypto, tradwife sexting, space travel app. It was originally LinkedIn, but he bought it and made a bunch of changes

---

*It's ya boi, Kevin. Yeah, I'm trying something new. What? My therapist said I need to be more assertive. Okay, I lied. It wasn't my therapist. It was my mom. But here goes: This Billionaire character is entirely fictional and not based on any real billionaires. Any similarities to a real billionaire's life should be interpreted as coincidental or as Mr. Torres Medina not being very imaginative.

everyone hated. Also, he fired most of the employees, and the others left. The only ones who remain are the immigrants. Not because of some great loyalty to the cause of replacing all communication with "69. Nice" jokes, but because the limiting conditions of your OPT and visas make it impossible to quit.

One morning, the Billionaire calls you into his office. He looks at you with those dead eyes of his and says in his weird accent, "Hey, I have a very important job for you." Skeptical of his intentions, you ask if it's okay if you continue your research into creating fully renewable, long-lasting hydrogen batteries. He says no. He needs you working on Project Tomorrow. You had heard about this, but thought it was a lie. It sounded too good to be true. The Billionaire and the world's greatest tech geniuses are getting together to find a way to terraform Mars, travel beyond the asteroid belt, and extend humanity beyond Tomorrow. You can't believe he actually wants you involved. Maybe the whole "idiot asshole who is also into authoritarians" was an act to throw people off the scent of his true intentions? This all feels a little too complicated, but hey, maybe his brain *does* work differently from yours and everyone else's. You nod. He presses a button with a giant sticker over it that says "The G Spot." A secret door opens behind his desk. He wants you to follow him. You do so and enter a long, dark tunnel. The Billionaire speaks to you as he carries a torch and guides the way. You realize he's not just speaking to you, he's practicing for when he gives this speech to the world.

"Project Tomorrow is the key to the survival of the human race. It is the last stronghold between human civilization and climate and economic disaster. In six weeks, the world will end. Climate devastation will erase every coastal city. Mount Everest will melt, creating landlocked tsunami avalanches. Every volcano in the world will go full-on Doctor Pimple Popper. Project Tomorrow is the world's greatest minds' reaction to this. We can't save every human. But we can save humanity. It is our best and only hope. It is the thing I dedicate most of my time to. That, and stealing memes from alt-right accounts about how FDR's polio vaccine created the My Lai Massacre, which was actually perpetrated by real-life Minions."

You nod. Okay, maybe he is crazy. Then he asks you for your honest opinion.

"What do you think of these?" the Billionaire asks as you emerge from the tunnel and you see them: three enormous spaceships, each the size of a football stadium, with quantum motors, cryo-sleep pods, and a Johnny Rockets on deck 14. Ships that will comfortably hold thousands of humans on a voyage across the stars in the search for our new home.

"They're . . . they're beautiful," you say.

"You don't think they aren't epicsauce enough?"

"No, no. They're incredible. I mean. I can't believe they're real."

"Oh, yeah. I came up with them myself," he says. "I think they're so funny."

"Funny?" Then you see it. You see what he's really pointing at. The names of the ships.

THE NINA

THE PINTA

THE SANTA MARIMJOB.

"It's like the ships that belonged to that cool guy who did nothing wrong, Columbus. But hilarious," he says. "It took me six months to think of that."

"Did you steal them off the Internet?" you ask.

"IT'S NOT STEALING IF I OWN THE SOCIAL MEDIA PLATFORM WHERE A POOR PERSON POSTED IT!" he observes.

"Right, sorry."

"So, do you like it?"

"The names or the ships?"

"The names. The ships were made by common nerds like you and slave labor from Myanmar. Did you know slaves existed for most of human existence and that slavery maybe is actually good, actually?" says the tech Billionaire.

"I guess."

"Okay, great. Your honesty will be rewarded."

You can't believe it. This is too much for one young person to comprehend. The world will end. Most people will die. But maybe you won't? Is he really offering you a place aboard one of the ships that will herald you and the remnants of humanity into a new age? You wonder what ship he will put you in. You hope it's not the Santa Marimjob. But your parents! And the rest of your family! All your friends! They won't make it. They probably will have to stay behind and learn how to live in a burning/constantly flooding world. They will have to learn how to grow dying crops and fight off radioactive six-foot-tall rats. You want to cry.

"I know it's a lot right now." says the Billionaire. "But for what it's worth, I think you deserve this. You know, as a thank you for the whole helping me name the ships thing."

He hands you something. You don't know what to say. Is it a keycard to your room on one of the ships? You realize your parents, your family, your loved ones would want nothing more than for you to be part of this brave new world. In your survival, they will live on. You will keep the memory of them—nay, the memory of Earth—alive. You will be the best colonist out there. You will do anything that is necessary to keep mankind alive. To keep *them* alive. You are ready to go.

"I am so grateful, sir," you say. "And whatever you need me to do on the ship, count me in."

"On the ship?" he asks. "Oh, no. Each one of those is for the future of mankind: a divorced billionaire. One is for me, and the other one is for Bezos."

"And the third one?" you ask.

"That's Bezos's space yacht's support space yacht. No, girl, no. My gift is a laser shank. It's like a *Star Wars* lightsaber but designed to fight off six-foot-tall radioactive rats. Anyway, thanks for the advice on the names. Toodles!"

He skips away and gets on the ship. A blast door closes behind him. No one and no thing is getting on that ship. The ships' quantum engines hum, and they start to leave the atmosphere. You watch as all three ships depart, leaving you stranded somewhere in America. Somewhere in Texas. Somewhere on a planet called Earth, where once we used to worry about things like visa statuses and borders and what happened on *The Bachelor*. Many years pass, and you sit by the kindling telling this story to your nephew, B3rt. You know it's the future because the E is a number. He asks you to tell him a story. Sweet B3rt. He is only five. He asks you to tell him the story of how you got the laser shank. You start at the beginning. As a young woman living in Argentina . . .

THE END

◆

YOU PROCURE YOUR FINANCIAL AID LESS THAN LEGALLY.

You join the local criminal underworld. It's a rough scene and not at all what you're used to, but you meet great, lifelong friends with incredible nicknames. Because in Latin American gangs, we get really creative with our nicknames, so they're not like Jimmy "Two Shoes" Fannelli. They're more like Eduardo "Biker Mouse from Mars" Tapia and "Alias Bimbo* Bread." Your criminal operation is extremely complicated: you smuggle bootleg region 4 DVDs to America. Turns out there's a huge revival for physical media after streaming services decided that the only way to make money was to delete entire movies off the Internet. Region 4 DVDs are exclusive to Latin America, the Caribbean, and Oceania, which means that if you have a region 4 DVD of *X-Men*, you get to hear Wolverine's actual Australian accent. Your job is to bring those DVDs to the United States so they can be sold to lonely nerds.

---

*Bimbo is a Mexican bread brand that operates all over Latin America, but it's also a very funny specific name.

After a few years working for Bimbo Bread's gang, you are finally given a solo assignment: travel to Houston, Texas, to deliver a suitcase full of copies of *Star Wars Episode II: Attack of the Clones*, but since it's a region 4 DVD, it's not called *Star Wars,* but rather *La Guerra de las galaxias,* which just translates to "Galaxy War" because us Latines are all about that drama. You feel ready for this. I mean, what could go wrong? What if you get caught? What is the worst thing that could happen if you get caught with a suitcase full of *Star Wars* DVDs?

You get caught by Border Patrol and you are accused of trying to destroy America. See, you got caught in that period of time where the *Star Wars* prequels had not been re-evaluated through the lens of nostalgia and were simply considered terrible movies. So, why would you bring so many copies of such a bad movie if not to corrupt the youth of America and destroy the nation? You are going to be sent to prison for a long, long time, but the prosecutors present you with a choice:

IF YOU REFUSE TO GIVE UP YOUR ENTIRE GANG
AND GO TO PRISON,

◆ TURN TO PAGE 84 ◆

IF YOU FLIP AND GIVE UP YOUR ENTIRE GANG,

◆ TURN TO PAGE 85 ◆

◆

YOU REFUSE TO GIVE UP YOUR ENTIRE GANG AND GO TO PRISON.

You go to prison, which most immigration lawyers can agree is bad. Sure, all your visas have been revoked, but since you're in federal prison, you're technically *living* in the US. So, in a sense, you've succeeded in your quest to move to the United States. Congrats!

You are mostly cooperative with the government. In prison, you learn that the inequalities that led you to a life of crime in your country are just as evident in the United States. You study hard and by the end of your sentence, you have become a published author and activist on social inequality.

You start getting invites to appear on morning shows and MSNBC. Unfortunately, you have to hang out with Joe Scarborough from *Morning Joe*. He wants you to listen to his band.

Crime truly doesn't pay.

THE END

◆

YOU FLIP AND GIVE UP YOUR ENTIRE GANG.

You rat everyone out and serve a rich-person sentence, like in that tennis prison from the end of *The Wolf of Wall Street*.

You sell your story to Netflix for millions of dollars, and it gets adapted into a show that casts a Brazilian as the mob boss from your country, which is not Brazil. Also Jared Leto has to wear a fat suit to play you.

You lose all your friends and never once stop to think about the inequalities that led them to a life of crime. And now you have to hang out with Jared Leto.

Crime truly doesn't pay.

THE END

♦

YOU KNOW WHO MORRISSEY IS.

Oh boy, do you like the arts. How's it going, buddy? Did you just Google a person you follow on Twitter who announced a career success and realize they're younger than you and now you feel like you're a talentless hack who will never amount to nothing? Good. Welcome to doing the thing you love. It sucks, and yet nothing feels better than actually doing this stupid thing you love. But, on the bright side, soon we will all be replaced by artificial intelligence designed and programmed by a group of people whose favorite book is something called *Hustle: The Beast Habits to Become a Business Megatron*, written by a guy who runs a crypto scam in Moldova.

You are the son of an upper-middle-class family in Bogotá, Colombia. You love writing and the arts. You are the only son of two doctors. Your mother is an ophthalmic surgeon, your father is a pediatrician. Your mother has always supported your dreams. Your father is a pediatrician. They are divorced.

You are finishing your degree in literature at Universidad de los Andes, often referred to as the "Harvard of Colombia" by no one except for alumni of the Universidad de los Andes who are so smug about having gone to Universidad de los Andes. It's a good school, and you meet friends who will last a lifetime, but you know you want to move to the US. Why? Because the US is the only country in the world that has the one thing you love: sitcoms. All the other countries give it a try, but save for a flash in the pan, phenomenal show from the UK or Ireland or Australia, no one has the record the US has. Just think, "What is the best television comedy from a country that isn't the US?" You can name maybe five. Here are just five US TV comedies: *The Brady Bunch*, *Parks and Recreation*, *SpongeBob SquarePants*, *Happy Days*, and *The Good Place*. They are all incredible TV shows that never won a Primetime Emmy Award and, save for *SpongeBob*, they're all off the air so they never will. This is kinda off topic, but it's crazy. *SpongeBob* has never won an Emmy. It's *SpongeBob*. From the memes! Which memes? ALL. OF. THEM. If this tangent feels self-indulgent in my own book, imagine how it felt at a Friday night house party with other kids who went to Universidad de los Andes. You were liked, but not well liked.

You decide to move to the US with the goal of becoming a television comedy writer. If your ancestors could hear you, they would say, "What is a television? And why are you speaking English? Can we please have some food? We are being murdered by the Conservatives." Unless they're from your mom's side of the family, in which case they'd say, "What is a television? And why are you speaking English? Can we please have some food? We are being murdered by the Liberals."

IF YOU WANT TO LEARN MORE ABOUT THE BLOODY
HISTORY OF COLOMBIA,

◆   CONTINUE TO THE NEXT PAGE   ◆

IF YOU ALREADY KNOW ABOUT THE BLOODY
HISTORY OF COLOMBIA,

◆   TURN TO PAGE 90   ◆

HISTORY OF COLOMBIA INTERLUDE

"Many years later, as he faced the firing squad, Colonel Aureliano Buendía was to remember the distant afternoon when his father took him to discover ice."

Oh my god, can you imagine if I included the entirety of *One Hundred Years of Solitude* here? I'd definitely hit my word count, but I think the ghost of Gabriel García Márquez would come to haunt me by constantly reminding me of how much of a better writer than me he is. He doesn't need to do that. His books already do that. Anyway, a good way to understand the violent history of Colombia is to go read *One Hundred Years of Solitude*. But don't be rude—finish this book first.

◆

YOU ALREADY KNOW ABOUT THE BLOODY HISTORY OF COLOMBIA.

You do your research and apply to several schools in the US. You're trying to get a master's degree in film and TV writing. Thankfully, there are many, many schools in the US that offer these in exchange for the very low price of $50,000 dollars for two years. You check your pockets to see if you have $50,000.

IF YOU MAGICALLY FOUND $50,000 IN YOUR POCKETS AND DO NOT REQUIRE FINANCIAL AID ANYMORE,

◆   **CONTINUE TO THE NEXT PAGE**   ◆

IF YOU DO NOT HAVE $50,000 IN YOUR POCKETS,

◆   **TURN TO PAGE 92**   ◆

♦

Whoa! You're *rich* rich! What are you doing? Are you a billionaire? Are you the grandchild of the richest man in Colombia, Julio Mario Santo Domingo? That means you are Tatiana Santo Domingo, also known as Tatiana Casiraghi, the wife of Andrea Casiraghi, fourth in the line of succession to the throne of Monaco. You just woke up in a fugue state where you thought you were a college kid who wanted to go to school in the United States. You call your security detail, and they fly you back to Monaco where you are seen by the best help money can buy, because again, you are literal royalty from fricking Monaco. After weeks of tests and exams the doctors agree it was a weird thing, but you can go back to doing princess of Monaco things like . . . starting fashion lines and . . . I'm gonna say . . . eating that one dish that only rich people know about: frenison. It's like venison, but it has wings and poops 100-Euro banknotes.

THE END

♦

YOU DO NOT HAVE $50,000 IN YOUR POCKETS.

You talk to your mom and decide to sell the one asset you have so you can pay for school. Your mom had bought an apartment when you were younger because real estate is the only safe investment. And now you've sold it. As a millennial, this means there goes your only chance at ever owning property. But this is your dream. Your American Dream. Sorry, this book is legally obligated to include the phrase "American Dream" at risk of deportation of the author. Of all the schools you applied to, you only get into one, but they're eager to have you and offer you an F-1 student visa.

WHAT IS AN

F-1 STUDENT VISA?

An F-1 visa is a student visa awarded to people attending university or college, high school, private elementary school, seminary, conservatory, and other academic institutions including language training programs. Duolingo does not count because it's not a real school, and because it's not really learning a language if all you're learning to say is, "The bear has a lot of mangoes."

You must prove that you are enrolled in a program or course that culminates in a degree, diploma, or certificate. So, you very much can get a visa to study at St. Bozo's Clown College of Clown, Improv, and Misplaced Investments, as long as you get a diploma for your degree in "performing to a crowd of five (5) people at 10 p.m. on a Wednesday." However, the school must be authorized by the US government to accept international students. So do your research before you apply to any random school. You don't want to end up at a place like Tufts. Tufts is authorized to accept international students, but it's Tufts.

FILING FEES

SEVIS (Student and Exchange Visitor)
Form I-90 Fee: **$350**

Form DS-160 Non-Immigrant Visa Application: **$160**

Other fees: **$150**

Tuition: **Full price! Most colleges and universities do not provide any sort of financial aid for international students.**

You go to the US Embassy for your US visa appointment. Most US embassies are located in the capital city of a country, but they don't all look alike. The one in Paris is a beautiful beaux-arts building right off the Place de la Concorde, while the one in Bogotá looks like a bunker, but it has an ice cream shop inside, so it's okay.

The problem with US embassies is that they are also the most terrifying places on Earth. See, when you apply for a visa, you're literally asking a random US citizen to look at a bunch of paperwork you had to print out and decide if you're actually telling the truth. Remember, you've already told them everything that's on the paperwork in a form they make you fill out online. That form times out if you spend too long looking through your entire home for your old passport to see if the last time you left your country was in 1997 or in 1998. Yeah, they ask that. Also, if the website times out, you have to start from scratch. It's like the myth of Sisyphus, but also, you may not be able to take your kids to Walt Disney World.

But here's the thing: even though you've already told them *when* you're flying to the US, *where* you plan on staying, and *how long* you plan on staying, and you've confirmed online that you are *not* part of a terrorist organization, they want you to print those answers out and bring them to your appointment. Along with everything from birth certificates to bank statements to, I guess, prove you've never kidnapped anyone? As the saying goes: there's nothing easier than proving a negative. So, as you can probably surmise, even the most gorgeous beaux-arts building feels terrifying if it's the one place where your entire future is in the hands of some guy named Keith.

You arrive at your visa appointment a full hour early. Why? Because if you're even a minute late, your application is void and you must start the entire process again. You realize that this is a pattern that you will see repeat itself more and more as your immigration journey continues: you are not allowed to make mistakes. This is the most treacherous adventure you could ever embark on. Like the guy from that video game *Pitfall*, every misstep can lead to extremely dangerous and potentially life-ending, well, pitfalls. Anyway, you arrive early and listen to a woman who works at the embassy as she reminds everyone to please have all their documents and their passport-sized photos ready to present at the entrance. You realize you didn't bring a physical copy of a passport photo. After all, why would you? You already uploaded a digital photo on the stupid website from hell, so why on Earth would they want a physical photo as well? But it is not your place to ask questions. You'll get to ask questions when you're a citizen.

Luckily, you live in Colombia, a nation of hard-working, resourceful people who will never let you down, as long as they're not playing for the men's soccer team, in which case, they will almost assuredly let you down. Your industrious compatriots have opened weird makeshift photo studios where you can get your picture taken before you even get in line to enter the embassy. You walk into the one closest to your place in line; a little hole-in-the-wall with a sign over the awning that reads "Photo America U.S.A." with a picture of a bald eagle, a US flag, Mickey Mouse, and, inexplicably, Bowser from *Super Mario*.

The place is no frills. You ask for two passport photos, and within ten minutes you are out of there, five thousand Colombian pesos poorer (in real money, a.k.a. US dollars, that's anywhere between one and three dollars, depending on the exchange rate), but you definitely have the damn photos. You arrive at the gate of the embassy and present your documents to a tall American man who pretends he doesn't speak Spanish because fuck you, that's why. He lets you into a narrow entrance where you must take off your shoes, jacket, wallet, and bags. It's all the glamour of going through airport security with zero Auntie Anne's pretzels waiting for you. But, when you think about it, it's also like a dress rehearsal for when you come to America and get the honor of going through TSA. One day, you daydream, you will be able to have your eczema cream taken from you and dumped in the trash because it's more than 3.4 ounces. Who cares if it's prescription? Not the TSA.

Once you're through security and they've made you store your phone in a locker, you wait in line. This is the first of many, many, MANY lines. See, the global network of US embassies is the only thing keeping the US line industry going. With the rise of FastPass, the line industry is dying, so it is your patriotic duty to stand in line at an embassy. After three different lines where three different employees repeatedly ask you the same questions, you finally reach the embassy agent who will decide if your visa gets stamped on your passport. Since it's very important to be able to communicate with them clearly, they only see you through bulletproof glass and talk to you over a prison phone. It makes you feel like they totally don't think you're a bad person who's definitely trying to come to their country to absolutely do bad things. You answer a couple of routine questions:

What is your name?

Felipe Torres Medina. Actually, Carlos Felipe Torres Medina, but Carlos is my dad's name and I kinda wanna do my own thing . . .

When were you born?

11/02/1991. Oh wait, no. That's in metric. Here's the American answer: 02/11/1991.

Where are you going to school?

Boston University.

How will you be able to afford tuition?

My mother sold the one piece of property we owned to be able to pay for my education. It's *very* immigrant chic.

Have you ever been to the US?

Yes, many times on tourist visas. [For more information on tourist visas, see opposite page.]

Have you recently lost two hundred pounds?

What?

Just answer the question, sir.

No?

You want to joke and say, "Omg, you noticed." But this is not the time for jokes. This is a serious embassy for serious people and serious visas. This is it. If you mess this up, you cannot move to the United States. And the truth is, you didn't lose 200 pounds. The man looks at you. He stares you down and decides you're telling the truth. He takes your passport and says they will stamp your visa and issue it in ten to fifteen days. He tells you to leave.

WHAT IS A
B-2 TOURISM VISA?

If you need to visit the US for a temporary stay, you can apply for a B-2 visa. It's what is commonly known as a tourist visa. It is what keeps the lights on at the USCIS, because every family who wants to go to Walt Disney World from 145 out of 195 countries needs to pay for a US tourist visa.

FUN FACT: The USCIS is one of the few agencies that stays open during government shutdowns because so many people come here and pay all sorts of fees, it basically funds itself.

You can apply for this visa yourself, but the most important thing is that you don't miss the interview in your home country. That's where a guy behind bulletproof glass makes sure you're not just going to stay in the US after you're done with your trip to the gem of New York City: the Times Square Bubba Gump Shrimp Company.
You can also enter the US on this visa if you're getting medical treatment, because it would be really evil to make you apply for another kind of visa when you're the kind of sick that

requires seeking medical treatment outside of your country. Must stop writing. Don't wanna give them any ideas.

FILING FEE

$185

And this is when you realize that there is a man, 200 pounds heavier than you, who has your same name and who might be a criminal. Now, this story is unconfirmed, and a lot of the record is gone, but this has to do with the fact that your official name in all your official documents is actually—like a lot of Latinos' first names—four names: a first name, a middle name, your father's last name, and your mother's last name. It means that you get to keep your heritage alive and that there's a plethora of permutations that allows you to have many namesakes. And that some of those namesakes might have committed crimes. And that those crimes might mean that you get flagged in the computer system that customs and border patrol officers use. In your years in America, you will try to learn the identities of several of those namesakes, and you will never know which one of them is the one who this particular officer thought you were.

After this, and for many years, every time you enter the United States, a border patrol officer will take your passport, ask for your fingerprints, take your picture, and, despite all the physical evidence that proves that you are who you are, and more importantly, proves who you are *not*, you will be taken to the border patrol back room. This is how you start learning about how, in the immigration system, you have to phrase everything like it's your fault. You have to say that you make things harder for myself by having four names. And, in one particular visit, the border patrol officer will ask you, "What'd you do that for? Give yourself four names." And you'll want to tell him that you didn't pick it. Because you don't really pick your own name. Your parents did. And you want to tell him about the Latin American tradition of having two last names. Torres and Medina are your last names. Torres belongs to your dad, and Medina to your mom. You also want to tell him about your mom's desire to give you a slightly different name than your father. Carlos is your dad's name, and since your mom didn't want you to be just Carlos Torres like him, she added the Felipe.

You'll want to say that, to clarify, your name is Carlos Felipe Torres Medina. That's the name on your passport. That's the name that you imagine pops a red flag on his system. You imagine there's a literal tiny red flag on the screen every time the officer does this, but you can't know because you are separated by thick glass, and his computer screen has that "no snooping" 3M plastic film over it. The US government will never tell you who the bad guy is who shares any combination of your names and makes the little red flag pop up. You do have this list of alleged criminals.* Maybe you've got it right:

Carlos Torres: Male, 37. Wanted by Modesto, California, police for murder committed on Nov. 23, 2003.

Carlos Torres: Male, 27. Wanted by Houston, Texas, police for murder and fleeing arrest in 2014.

Carlos Torres: Male, 34. Registered sex offender.

Felipe Torres: Male. Real name, Carlos Arturo Velandia. Former Colombian guerrilla leader.

Carlos Medina: Male. Victim of murder in Kodiak, Alaska.

You wonder if, were you to find the person whom they mistake you for every time you come into the United States, would you be able to get them to tell the government that they're not you? But you don't say any of these things. You just follow the man into the back room. The back room is not a horrible interrogation room like the

---

*Um . . . this is Kevin. Save for the guerrilla leader, these criminals are fake, but there are some people who have broken the law who share combinations of names with the author of this book. But we are not gonna put a list people's crimes on blast for a joke book.

ones you see in the movies, with the fake mirrored glass. It's just like a worse-lit DMV, and instead of people waiting to get their driver's licenses, there are people waiting to see if they can enter the land of the free and the home of the brave. You sit there, waiting for them to call your name after they have confirmed what their eyes and ears have told them: that you are not the person whom you are not.

When the officer calls your name, you want to ask him a couple of questions. Namely:

1. Could you not make fun of my situation if it indeed does happen again? Don't say stuff like, "Every time? It sure sucks to have your name" or "Blame your momma and poppa" (which you did). Maybe you're just trying to be nice, but when you're all in uniform and have my passport with my student visa, all my documentation, and all my info, it's a bit scary.

2. Could you not attempt to make small talk about the Hulu show *11.22.63*, based on a Stephen King novel, while you hold my documents? Also, could you not wave all my documents around in your hand as you explain to me why the book's ending is "crap"?

3. Could you not take me to the back room with all the actual criminals? I'm a nerdy kid from Latin America—not any of the guys listed earlier.

4. If you *have* to take me into the back room, could I be allowed to text? Like I said: I'm a nerdy kid from Latin America.

You do not ask any of these, but you do find a sliver of courage and try to ask a question. However, since you're a smarty pants (the F-1 student visa proves it), you frame the question as something *you* can do. You don't ask, "Can you leave a note in the system so you don't have to bring me into this stupid room again?" You say, "Is there anything *I* can do, so that *your* job is easier, and you don't have to waste time by bringing me here?" And he responds in an almost too typical Brooklyn accent, "Change your name! Find a good Jewish girl and marry her. This wouldn't happen if your name was Carlos Schwartz!"

First of all, that's very progressive! He assumes you, a man, will change your name for your future wife! That said, you don't know anyone with that last name yet, so maybe you should ask the officer if he can introduce you to a nice young lady with that last name. You don't, because you're scared of the border patrol officer, and after that encounter, you will go back to your temporary home, the place where you're going to school: a ~~village~~—sorry you're supposed to call it a city—called Boston.

IF YOU ARE FROM BOSTON OR THE NEW ENGLAND AREA AND ARE SENSITIVE ABOUT PEOPLE DUNKING (DUNKIES?) ON BOSTON AND NEED AN EMOTIONAL SUPPORT SECTION OF JOKES DUNKING ON NEW YORK CITY,

◆　　CONTINUE TO THE NEXT PAGE　　◆

IF YOU KNOW THE TRUTH—THAT BOSTON SUCKS—

◆　　TURN TO PAGE 107　　◆

HERE'S AN EMOTIONAL SUPPORT SECTION OF JOKES DUNKING ON NEW YORK CITY

Ah! New York City! The city so nice, they only discovered trash dumpsters in the year 2023. They say that if you can make it there, you can make it anywhere. You assume "it" means public urination. It's the perfect city for anyone who's ever said, "I love walking, I just wish there were more psycho cab drivers trying to run me over while I do it." And the subway. What a wonder of modern urban achievement. Did you know that the New York City subway transports, on average, about 3.6 million people every day? That's like four mariachi bands. And don't get me started on New York's sports teams. No, really, don't, because I don't know much about them other than the Mets are bad in a sports way and the Yankees are bad in a non-sports way. People say New York is dangerous, and it's true: New York is home to some of the most dangerous people on Earth—NYU kids. Either they are very talented and are more successful than you, or they are not at all talented and are more successful than you. Those are the scariest ones of them all. They are relentless. They will find you at a party, then follow you home, and just when you think you've outrun them, they'll show up at your stoop and start telling you about the movie they shot over the summer. They didn't really need funding because the lead is their classmate, who is also the son of the top agent at an entertainment firm. The movie also doesn't really have a plot, but since their writer—their other classmate—is the grandson of an original SNL cast member (no, not that one), it's already in the festival circuit. Actually, it's already been purchased by a production company. Actually, it's now a show on Peacock. It's been greenlit for two seasons. He's also itching to give you notes on your book about immigration. His father isn't an immigrant, but he's pretty sure his dad's assistant is. Her name is . . . Rosario? Nope. That's just the maid from *Will & Grace*.

Okay. Now stop being a baby, admit that Boston sucks, and

◆ CONTINUE TO THE NEXT PAGE ◆

♦

YOU KNOW THE TRUTH—THAT BOSTON SUCKS.

You want to like Boston. You really do. But the truth is that you don't. There are some pretty good things about Boston, like . . . the movie *The Departed* and . . . you assume other things. You like the school you go to. You like your teachers. You like your classmates. At least, not the ones who keep asking you if you swam from South America. But it just . . . doesn't feel like home. It's not Boston's problem that you don't like it (Boston's problems are way too many to be enumerated in this book, but just two big ones come to mind: racism and the Green Line). It's your problem. You want to take Boston out to dinner—in the North End, because you're classy—and tell it, "It's not you, it's me." And Boston will probably agree, because of the aforementioned racism. You learn a lot during your time in Boston: about screenwriting, but also about the US, and about yourself. After your two years in Boston, you can say that you learned three things: the three-act structure of screenplays; the fact that Americans love immigrants as long as they're Canadians, like Ryan Reynolds; and that you love pad see ew. As soon as you graduate, however, you are ready to move to a real city. And thankfully, you have OPT.

TO LEARN ABOUT OPT,

◆   TURN TO PAGE 50   ◆

◆

YOU HAVE OPT AND YOU'RE NOT
A STEM STUDENT.

You choose to move to New York City, the home of Liz Lemon, Spider-Man, and all the dead bodies from *Law & Order*. You move into a room in an apartment in Astoria that you found through a friend who also does improv. Oh yeah, you do improv too.* As an artistic spirit, you have always felt drawn to New York. It's a real city. It has Broadway and the Statue of Liberty and the Drama Book Shop and The Strand, and it's where, when you were nine years old, you tried your first Quarter Pounder with Cheese because there wasn't a single McDonald's in Colombia at the time. It is America. And, as a person interested in working in movies and television and, specifically,

---

*I know. That's probably the cruelest fate I could've subjected you to as an author, but I never said anything about these stories was easy. You do improv. Worse, you like improv. A lot. You will willingly spend several hours of your life in the basements of bars and the basements of art galleries and the basements of restaurants and in other assorted fire hazards pretending to give birth to Colonel Sanders, and you will love it.

comedy, it's special because it's where the *Late Show with David Letterman*, *The Tonight Show*, *Conan*, and *SNL* are taped.

A few years into the future, on one of those New York summer nights that are just perfect, before the air gets all muggy and before the trash begins to really smell, you will be walking up 26th Street and Broadway and a pedestrian light will force you to stop right by a family of tourists. They will look up and see the Empire State Building: the symbol of our city and the bane of our King Kongs. They will stare in awe, and so will you. Then one of them will tell the others in his group, with the confidence only white men have, "That's the Empire State Building." He will pause so his friends can properly take in the moment and then say, "It's where they record *SNL*."* And they will be so impressed, and you won't say anything about how he's so wrong because you know what? This is New York City, and yeah, that's where they tape *SNL*. New York needs the myths and lies we tell ourselves about it. Not because it would stop being a massive metropolis and the world capital of finance, but rather because without them it would only be another massive metropolis full of finance bros. It would be no different from Chicago or, worse, London. So yeah, *SNL* is taped at the top of the Empire State Building on the observation deck, which is also where Tom Hanks and Meg Ryan live. And Lady Liberty is dating Rockefeller Center, but, on the DL, she's having a hot affair with the Wall Street Bull. And that one taxi you saw is the taxi from *Taxi Driver*, and that street right next to your unlicensed Airbnb is definitely where Harry met Sally, and that guy you saw eating dim sum in that public park in Chinatown who you're pretty sure is Spike Lee *is* Spike Lee. Also, Tom's Restaurant is the actual restaurant from

---

*It is not. *SNL* is taped in 30 Rockefeller Plaza, the main building in Rockefeller Center.

Seinfeld, even the interiors, and your dad, who was excited to take you there, is right, they actually shot the show there and probably just redid the inside. New York is awesome. In the real sense of the word and in the millennial, slangy sense. And you live here.

You live in Queens, which, for anyone who doesn't live in New York, fucking rules. It's the largest, most populous borough and it has everything you could ever need, except a subway line that connects it to Brooklyn because Robert Moses was an incredible racist. As you live longer in America, you start to realize that most infrastructure failings in the country—and, to be fair, in most Western developed countries—happened because architects and city planners with impressive degrees just could not fathom the idea of having to drive by the place where an Irishman, a Nigerian, or a Mexican lived. That makes it pretty hard for you to get to your job at a production company in Brooklyn. That's the fancy way to describe it. Because what it really is, is the guerrilla film studio set up in a basement. It's far and the hours are long, but at least it is also *far* and the hours are long. Also, it doesn't pay.

As you contemplate if purchasing a fifth can of tuna for the month is a financial decision from which you will never recover, you wonder if this is one of those jobs you—an immigrant—stole from an American. You get the can of tuna and decide that the only way to survive is to pull yourself up by your bootstraps and find a new source of income. You're a young millennial with a gift for writing. In fact, you've entered a few writing competitions over the summer and done pretty well. You didn't win either of them, but one of your screenplays was a semifinalist in a competition, and one of your short stories was a finalist in a contest judged by your literal favorite author. Yeah! You've got talent! So, you will do what so many millennials have done before you: you will find a way to make money . . . by blogging.

Thankfully, you move to New York in the golden age of content media websites that are, in their own words on their "About us" page, actually "upending what we understand as journalism and media as a whole." That's millennial VC horsecrap for: "We can hire a bunch of freelance writers and, because they're under 26, they won't know they don't have health insurance until it's too late. And when they ask about benefits, we'll just give them pizza and tell them the office is pet-friendly. Who cares if the CEO's dog pissed on your leg! This wouldn't happen at a stupid corporate job!"

The company you work for is called something like HypeYASSS. It is very popular. People say it's only a hub for mindless online quizzes written by morons, like "Which Disney Princess Are You Based on Your Data, Please Give Us Your Data." But this is 2015. They have a burgeoning and exciting news division that hired some pretty talented and interesting people. Of course, by the time this book is published, HypeYASSS will have obliterated their news division and shifted their business model entirely to online quizzes written poorly by AI, like "Which Disney Princess Are You Based on Your Data, Please Give Us Your Data."

As crazy as it sounds, there was a moment in time where there was a publication called something like HypeYASSS News and they went to the White House Correspondents' Dinner and everything, and people actually took it seriously because, to be fair, some very talented people worked there, but it still had a ridiculous name. Unfortunately, and as much as you would like to join the cool kids in the news division, you are stuck writing listicles for HypeYASSS Español. You're happy to do it because HypeYASSS actually pays, but it's hard to be creatively fulfilled when your assignments are things like "20 Times the Colombian Police's Twitter Account Was Giving Us Life." While your job may not be the job you imagined when you thought of being a writer in New York, it is somehow . . . cool. People tell you your job is cool. And you start believing it. At the time, you're single and in New York. You're broke, but something you discover is that freelancing for HypeYASSS is kind of a cool thing to do. This doesn't make you more successful on dates, because a long-term relationship with a person who did not love you and cheated on you repeatedly has obliterated any sense of self-worth you have. But when you do go on dates, and the dates ask you what your job is, you say, "I actually write for HypeYASSS." And they respond, "Oh, wow. Cool!" in a genuine way that isn't the polite way in which we all say "Oh, wow. Cool!" when we ask our co-worker's husband what his job is, and he says he works in "finance" or "I'm a lawyer for a bank."

And since you start buying into the hype about HypeYASSS, there's nothing you want more than to be able to work there full time. Plus, your OPT is running out, and since you're in the arts, you don't have a lot of time. HypeYASSS is exactly the kind of pluralist, hyper-young, super-progressive company that will sponsor your visa. Some of the people you work with also come from other countries. For all you know, HypeYASSS is the first step on your way to conquering America. Not in an Attila the Hun way, but rather in a Taylor Swift way—as an undeniable talent who will singlehandedly keep the economy afloat before her eventual transformation into the benevolent overlord we all yearn for. That's why you are thrilled when your editor informs you there is a full-time job opening at HypeYASSS Español that you'd be perfect for. You apply for it, and after three rounds of interviews, you get a call from your editor. You interviewed with them. You know them. They like you. Which is why you're sure this is the call that's gonna change your life. You'll start working at HypeYASSS full time, and you'll get noticed by the News Division. You will create content so viral and hilarious that *The Daily Show* will not be able to ignore you. You will become a correspondent and eventually get your own spin-off show, like *The Colbert Report*, but better. Because . . . well, you haven't really thought of the specifics of why it would be better. Or what your character traits would be as a correspondent. You've mostly daydreamed about being a correspondent on *The Daily Show* while sitting in improv class, not really paying attention to the scene your classmates are performing because one of them is a young woman who has never even attempted to listen to her scene partner and the other one is a 57-year-old man who unironically called you "a Mexican." So, you pick up the phone and listen to your editor as she tells you that unfortunately they will not be able to hire you. "But don't worry," she says. "It's not because we don't think you'd be perfect for the job. It's because HypeYASSS is eliminating the entire HypeYASSS Español division." Apparently, not making any money is bad for business! You say you understand and hang up. You're devastated. This was it. This was your chance to stay. You begin to spiral. Not literally, but after a few minutes you do feel like you want to puke. The clock is ticking and there is no way you'll have enough time to develop a relationship with a company big enough and willing enough to get you a work visa. Also, it's an election year and the guy who called Mexicans rapists is hosting *SNL*. The show you love. He is hosting it. And people love him. Even though he hates you. You can't believe they let him host *SNL*. You are so mad, but at least you know that being the host of *SNL* is definitely the highest position Donald Trump will ever hold, and he will surely never, ever be able to shape immigration policy.

Since you still have your job at the production company, you aren't in violation of your OPT, but you do have a couple days off every week because people don't really want to hire you with your OPT running out, and because once a week you were supposed to go to the HypeYASSS office where you are now *persona non grata*. That's Latin, not Español, but since they got rid of their Español division, they wouldn't know the difference. One of your favorite bands, Vampire Weekend, will be performing at a Washington Square Park rally for Bernie Sanders.* You show up to the rally, but realize that you're not the only 22-year-old in the vicinity of NYU who wants to see Bernie Sanders and Vampire Weekend. You try to get close to the park but realize there's a line that starts all the way by The Strand bookstore, on 13th Street. For those who aren't acquainted with Manhattan, that is one block south of another public park/ meeting square for political rallies, Union Square, where another rally is happening. Since it's Union Square, that rally could be anything from protesting/supporting tariffs on Venezuelan politicians to protesting/supporting a man's right to get circumcised. But, to put that in perspective, the line to attend one rally is getting so long, it's about to become its own rally. You get in line and absentmindedly check Facebook. That's where you see that your friend from improv, Robin, has posted that she also plans on going to the rally. You message her because you want to hang, and definitely because you're hoping she's farther forward in the line and maybe she can cut you in. She is not. In fact, she hasn't arrived at either park yet. You tell her the line is crazy, and she asks if, instead of going to this political rally, you wanna grab a drink. You say yes.

---

*This is a real thing that happened. This is also the most 2015 liberal, millennial, coastal elite sentence you will ever read in your life. I tried to engineer a more liberal, millennial, coastal elite sentence in a science computer lab, and it didn't work. I broke the computer and all it would come up with was the line "What if Obama was LCD Soundsystem" over and over and over again.

This is a small aside in the book where I want to break the illusion that this is your story and want you to hear directly from me, the author, Felipe. I know this is confusing and you're thinking "Wait, I am Felipe. That's what the past couple of pages told me." But bear with me for a second. The path you've been reading up till now is, for the most part, true—the broad strokes, anyway. Unlike the other stories in the book, which are exaggerated for comedic effect, this is stuff that happened to me. That is why I need you to know that the sentence that will come after this paragraph is not a joke. It is not an invention or exaggeration added for comedic effect. It is not an emotional truth. It is THE truth. It is an objective thing that happened. It happened on April 13, 2016. I am not making this up. Okay, here it goes:

Your life is about to change forever because you agreed to go to a skeleton-themed restaurant in the West Village called Jekyll and Hyde.

The location you went to is now out of business, but the best way to describe Jekyll and Hyde is like if Chuck E. Cheese replaced the animatronic animal band with underpaid actors pretending to be unlicensed spooky monsters. And the reason your life will change is because you're hanging out with an immigrant who knows more than you. See, Robin is Dutch, and she's been in the United States for several years. She's also an actor and a very successful voice actor.* And while another actor pretending to be some sort of steampunk Doctor Frankenstein serves you a plate of chicken wings ("booooo-ne

---

*And she told me I wouldn't have to change her name for the book as long as I mentioned she is—in her own words—"like God but better, and with a better haircut."

116

in") to share, you tell her everything about HypeYASSS and about how you don't think you'll be able to stay in the US because no company will sponsor a work visa for you. Because she's a good improv scene partner, she listens. And then she says the words that will change your life: "Have you thought of getting an O-1 visa?" You laugh. Of course you've thought about it. But you don't have an Oscar or an Emmy or a Nobel Prize or enough money to buy a Grammy. So, you tell her the truth, that you don't think you could get it. She disagrees. Because, see, she doesn't have any of those awards either, but she has an O-1 visa. You start to think that maybe you don't know what exactly an O-1 visa is.

WHAT IS AN

O-1 VISA?

An O-1 is a nonimmigrant visa, which basically is every kind of visa except for the ones that help you settle in the United States permanently. Republicans' ultimate wish, of course, is to get rid of nonimmigrant visas and replace them with no-immigrant visas, which will finally rid the immigration system of those pesky immigrants. Problem solved.

O-1 visas allow certain individuals to come to work in the US without any sort of lottery system, but to avoid the traditional work visa issues, you must prove you have extraordinary abilities. So, you're a shoo-in if you attend Xavier's School for Gifted Youngsters, although if you are going to school, you probably have an F-1 visa. What? Do you not think the X-Men had to think about visas? They *definitely* had to deal with annoying immigration stuff. Storm is Kenyan, Nightcrawler is German, and Wolverine is Canadian. Yeah, Wolverine is from Alberta. All of a sudden, the Adamantium claws are way less intimidating when you have to imagine they come from a guy who says, "Sorry aboot that, bub. I have to go to my heuse to watch the Canadiens game. I got some money with the Queen's face on it. Not that much, just a couple of loonies and toonies." Magneto is from Poland. However, Magneto doesn't worry about visas because he just uses his badass magnetic powers to break all the rules, but that's okay. Magneto was, is, and always will be right.

The government allows you to apply for an O-1 visa if you want to prove your extraordinary abilities in:

- Arts (like Adele, singer, roller in the deep)
- Sciences (like Elizabeth Blackburn, Nobel Prize–winning molecular biologist)
- Athletics (like Lionel Messi, boy who is good at ball)
- Education (like Harvard medievalist Nicholas Watson. What? You don't know him? You rube.)
- Business/Entrepreneurship (like Mark Cuban. What do you mean he's not Cuban? He's from Pittsburgh? But his name is "Cuban.")

You can also get an O-1 visa if you can prove that you have a demonstrated record of extraordinary achievement in the motion picture or television industry and have been recognized nationally or internationally for those achievements. Like the writer of this book, Felipe Torres Medina. He is so great. He has a Peabody Award, a Writers Guild of America Award, and more than five Emmy nominations. Did you also know he's very handsome?

Ok, enough funny business, let's get down to real business.

What do you need to get an O-1 visa?

- You need a petitioner, who is someone in the US to be your American avatar. That means: a prospective employer, your accountant, a lawyer, or a good friend who wants to save an immigrant. They do not have to be avatars from the movie *Avatar*. In fact, they can't be avatars because they're not American. They are Na'vi. Your petitioner can be a US citizen, US company, or lawful permanent resident (so, a green card holder).

Note: If your petitioner is your prospective employer, then you can only work for that employer.

- Ten letters of intent for potential employment from foreign and domestic employers to show you'll have stuff to do during the three years you're granted this visa. Basically, contracts for gigs or work you will perform in America for three years, which is easier for professors or scientists, but a bit harder in the arts, unless you land a residency in Vegas, like Adele.
- Beneficiary and petitioner documents. That's just legal talk for LOTSA FORMS.
- Evidence of extraordinary ability—this is the real stuff.
  - Your resume/work history.
  - Letters of recommendation from people in your field who know your work and can vouch for you. These letters have to say you're, like, the most important, wonderful person in the world and that America needs your vital work in tech/medicine/ the 100-yard dash/interpretative shadow puppets.
  - News clips about you. The good kind, not the "Florida man" kind.
  - Stories where you were interviewed as an expert in your respective field.
  - Awards (Do you have an Emmy? Well good fucking for you. I don't. I'm the Colombian with most

nominations ever, but I guess John Oliver and his writers need another one.)

- ○ Acclaimed projects where you had an integral role (e.g., were you ever a judge on a hottest hockey player competition? Were you ever a judge for an incubator program looking for useless startups?)

Once this is out of the way, you're all good!

Oh, sorry, I meant, you need more stuff. Specifically, what the government calls an "advisory opinion" (or two or more).

The law requires that a consultation letter or a letter of no objection be provided by a labor organization, peer group, and/or, in some cases, a management organization (so it helps if your profession has a guild or union or council of elders in weirdo robes who can certify you're an alien of extraordinary ability). Also, it's not free; depending on your field, each organization charges from $200 up to $600 to write such a letter.

So, once all of that is out of the way, then you have the privilege of paying about $500 ($460 as of December 2023) to apply for your visa. If you don't want to wait months for a response, you can pay an extra $2,500 premium processing fee to get your result in two weeks.

But okay, once you have all that stuff, you're done, right? You have your visa, right? Wrong! All these documents and paperwork and stress are sent to a single USCIS agent who decides your fate. Just one guy or gal! They get to decide if you actually have extraordinary ability. Fun, huh?

FILING FEES

Application Fee: **$460**

Premium Processing Fee: **$2,500**

Legal Fees: **$5,000–$10,000**

You decide you'll find an immigration lawyer and apply for an O-1B visa to be recognized as an Alien of Extraordinary Ability in the Arts. It is impossible to get this visa without an immigration lawyer, so from the get-go that's at least $2,000 to $3,000 you'll have to come up with. Minimum. Around the same time, you score a gig to work as a bilingual copywriter at an ad agency in Manhattan. It's very hip, there are donuts in the break room almost constantly, and there's a basketball hoop in the middle of the loft that has been converted into an office. It's not so much *Mad Men* as it is Grown-ass Men who collect Funko Pop! figures, but it's cool. The people are nice, it pays okay, and, most importantly, it lets you quit the production company job. You don't have any experience in advertising or any education in it either, but you speak Spanish and you worked at HypeYASSS, so you definitely know the arcane magicks required to make things go viral. It's so easy to replicate viral content. That's why every one does it all the time and we all know the secret to it.

You make your mark quickly by deftly finding user-generated content on Instagram and asking the users if you can reshare it from the Twitter account of a cable company. But since Twitter still has a 140-character limit, you're kind of like a modern-day Hemingway. But better. After a short time, you've graduated from writing for the cable company and are allowed to write real ads for very cool clients, like fancy French spirits brands and a national sports league. Not the big one, but no, not hockey. It's soccer. You write for Major League Soccer. You know their slogan: "We call it soccer, but half of our teams have the words 'Football Club' in their name to confuse the fans."

During some sort of post-work drink gathering, you mention your visa application, and a coworker who is from another country (one of the ones in the MEDIUM difficulty in this book), says the company can hire a lawyer to get you an O-1 visa. That's how he got his visa, and he's in America, so you know the lawyer must be good. Also, the company would pay for it. You can't believe it. You've hit the jackpot. Once again, talking to other immigrants has reaped immense benefits. The main one here: not having to pay your immigration lawyer out of pocket. He says he'll talk to the legal department at the agency (a.k.a. one woman of color who happens to be both the legal and payroll departments, and also HR?????) and he'll "get your visa sorted in two weeks" because the agency will pay for premium processing. The things money can get you in this country. Sorry, that wasn't a rhetorical expression. It was a Jeopardy category. "I'll take 'the things money can get you in this country' for $2,000, Ken." The answer: What are most things?

You email the lawyer you had personally procured, and he totally understands you dropping him. In fact, he congratulates you for being able to get the visa situation handled by your company. The next day, you meet the new lawyer, who is—and this is no exaggeration or creative embellishment—the meanest person you will ever meet. She simply does not like you. She tells you there's no way you're getting this visa, but that she'll send your application to the government because she's still getting paid. You diligently get all the paperwork to her, which you had for the most part already procured for your other lawyer. She responds by berating you for only having eight letters of recommendation instead of ten. You start to freak out, but as you scroll through a seven-hundred-page slideshow deck containing all your life's work and achievements to prove to the government you deserve to stay, you remember that story that was judged by your favorite author.

There's no way, right? There's no way in this labyrinth that we call the immigration system, in this system that saddled you with a lawyer that laughs at your attempts to stay in the country, that you will be able to just cold-email a MacArthur Genius Grant winner, who also happens to be your favorite living author, who has not met you in person, asking for a letter of recommendation, and they're just gonna say yes. I mean, he's a very good and famous and busy writer! There's no way he checks the one email address you found publicly available on the Internet, right? No way. And the truth is he might not. But that day was the one day he had to change his email password for work, and so he was logged on and he saw your email. The fact that your email wasn't sent to spam or that he didn't immediately dismiss it as spam does not and should not escape you. Because, as you learn the longer you stay here, the truth is that being an immigrant in the United States takes a lot of work and a lot of time and a lot of money. But it also takes a tremendous amount of luck and generosity of people who just choose to be kind. A few days after sending your email asking for his help, you have a beautiful letter written and signed by your favorite author, saying it's a good thing for this country that you're here. In the future, you will show this letter to a girl that you like on your first date. You do carry the letter around, but not because you're a narcissist. You carry it around in a big, overstuffed folder in your backpack that you take everywhere you go because you are paranoid the police will stop you and ask for your papers and you'll have to explain your entire visa application, and so you carry that seven-hundred-page document with you at all times. You know showing her the letter can read as very douchey, but you like her. And she likes the letter. And, more importantly, she likes you. You will marry her. But that's later.

You send the letter to the mean lawyer and feel pretty proud of yourself. This is a letter of recommendation from a very well-regarded and very well-known author. That means you're a shoo-in. This is a home run! A touchdown! A whatever you call scoring a point in lacrosse! You tell your lawyer you got a letter from the author, hoping she will finally say, "Oh, this really helps your case." But, instead, she just responds, "Who?" Then, she submits the visa application with premium processing.

Two weeks later, as promised, you get a response from the government. It's not a yes. And that's when you have your first panic attack. You've never had a panic attack before, so all you know is that you can't really breathe, that there are obviously a million ants running up and down your arms, that your legs have turned into noodles, and that you actually were never able to see before. It's all pitch black. No one notices at work because half of the agency is shooting a commercial, and the other half sits on the other side of the loft by the basketball hoop.

After a few minutes, you realize you must've been moving on autopilot because you're standing somewhere in Chelsea, breathing heavily and leaning against some scaffolding. You call the lawyer and ask what can be done. She says the government didn't outright reject your case, but rather sent you a "Request for Evidence." You say, "Oh, well, that's a good thing, right? I mean, it's better than getting rejected, right?" And she says they don't really issue outright rejections, so you shouldn't read into it as a positive. You think something along the lines of, "Wow, even now she has zero empathy. There is truly no way she could be a meaner lawyer." She then tells you that she warned you you weren't going to get this visa. She says, "There are people who've been to the Olympics that don't get this visa." You say you understand and hang up. You call your mom. You cry. A big part of being an immigrant is calling your mom. Another big part of being an immigrant is crying. Most days you only do one of the two. When you do both at the same time, it usually means something has gone horribly wrong or wonderfully right.

You give yourself an afternoon to be sad. You buy a bottle of vodka—you don't even like vodka—and the most American food you can think of: Taco Bell. You try to escape your reality by doing your favorite thing: watching comedy on television. The problem is, you can't really enjoy it because the reason you're sad is that you feel like you'll never be able to fulfill your dream of writing comedy for television. So, emboldened by that dream and the entire bottle of vodka, you open the email containing the Request for Evidence. If there's one thing you can do, it's tell the government how dumb they're being. So, you start annotating it. The RFE contains all the grounds for why your application was not accepted. You have to hand it to the USCIS: they read the entire application. That's probably what hurts the most. That they saw all your work and said "nah." But you're nothing if not persistent. In fact, you're pretty annoying. So, you go over every single instance where they found you lacking and mark up the PDF with your arguments for why you *do* qualify. You think, "This might be the vodka talking, but *Вы определенно имеете право на эту чертову визу*!" which, according to Google Translate, means, "You definitely qualify for the damn visa!" You're so mad. And she's so mean. And the USCIS is so wrong. They must be. You realize you're going to need a second opinion. Preferably an un-vodka-fied opinion.

The next day, you email your other lawyer. The one you'd hired out of your own pocket. You let him know about the RFE. You ask if you could re-hire him. If he could contest the RFE. He says yes and asks to see what the government said. You expect him to take a few days to pore over the document to find how you will argue your case. He responds ten minutes later. He says there's a problem with the application for your O-1B visa. "It appears your lawyer filed for an O-1A visa."

Yes. The mean lawyer filed for the wrong kind of visa. And yes, she got paid for it.

WHAT IS AN
O-1A VISA?

All the stuff you read for an O-1 visa still applies, but only to individuals with "extraordinary ability in the sciences, education, business, or athletics." So if you're a hot Canadian hockey player, a very hot basketball player, a not-so-hot tech bro who believes in effective altruism, or a hot teacher (?), then you may qualify for an O-1A. This is a three-year visa that can be extended in 1-year increments or reapplied to for additional three-year periods.

The ways in which you prove your extraordinary abilities are:

- Awards! Big ones count, of course, but also small ones from your country.
- Have you judged other people in your science or tech or business field? Like, not as in legal justice, but like in a contest or competition? Are you one of the sharks in your country's *Shark Tank*? If so, congrats—that counts!
- Published materials recognized in major trade publications. So an article in *Science* or *The New England Journal of Medicine*, or, if you're in business, *Fleece Patagonia Vest Weekly*.
- Original scientific, scholarly, athletic, or business contributions of significance in your field. Did you

invent that thing soccer players do where they cover their balls when they're defending a free kick? Put it in your application.

- Are you an essential member in an organization or a club that is important to your field? Sorry, Groucho Marx. Being in clubs is actually helpful.
- Dolla dolla billz. Or Euro Euro Notez. Or Dinar Dinar Notez. If you make a high salary or a higher salary than others in your field, that counts.

Seeing as you're not an athlete or a scientist or a scholar, it actually tracks that you wouldn't qualify for a visa for athletes, scientists, or scholars.

Unless . . .

IF YOU'VE SECRETLY BEEN AN ELITE-LEVEL ATHLETE THIS WHOLE TIME,

◆   TURN TO PAGE 132   ◆

IF YOU HAVE NOT SECRETLY BEEN AN ELITE-LEVEL ATHLETE THIS WHOLE TIME,

◆   TURN TO PAGE 148   ◆

♦

YOU'VE SECRETLY BEEN AN ELITE-LEVEL ATHLETE THIS WHOLE TIME.

Whoa! You've been holding out on us. Since you are an elite-level soccer player, and the ad agency you've been working for instead of being a millionaire soccer player works with Major League Soccer, you figure you'll pay them a visit. You show up at their offices without invitation and say, "Until yesterday, I was trying to make my way in America as some sort of artist, like a fricking moron. But now, I will prove to you all that I am the next greatest soccer player of all time. Pelé? More like Pe-LAME. Messi? Yeah, he's sloppy on the ball compared to me. Johan Cruyff? Yeah, he's gonna Cruy tears of joy after seeing me play. Yeah, I know I'm not pronouncing Cruyff's name right to make that dig, but Johan Cruyff can't do anything about it. Because he's dead." The receptionist, who is certainly terrified of you and perhaps hoping you'll leave, tells you there's an open call training that weekend in New Jersey.

You attend and it turns out you're not the next Messi, but you're good enough to be hired by Columbus Crew, a real-life Major League Soccer team based in Columbus, Ohio. Of all the cities in Ohio, it's certainly one of the three that starts with a "C." Isn't that weird? Cleveland, Columbus, and Cincinnati all start with a "C." There's no illuminati conspiracy at play here, but it's weird, right? Imagine if the three major cities in Florida were Miami, Mampa, and Malahassee. You'd be like, "huh!"

You move to Columbus, and while you ride the bench for a lot of the season, the team welcomes you with open arms. Your O-1A visa is approved within two weeks because Columbus Crew and Major League Soccer have a team of lawyers who are very good at getting visas for foreign players and are not mean. You have a decent first season, but Columbus barely qualifies to the MLS Cup, and it's a little bit your fault. Here's what happened: You're in the locker room surrounded by your beautiful fellow soccer jock boys after training. You're all discussing what you're going to do to prepare for the big game tomorrow. Your teammate jokingly says, "I'm gonna hit up Sonic." And everyone but you laughs. The other beautiful soccer boys notice and because they are sweet, sensitive boys, they ask you why you're not laughing. After months of camaraderie and joint triumph, you feel you can be honest with them. "My fellow beautiful soccer boys," you say, "the reason I am not laughing is because I don't understand why this is a joke. Because . . . I have never been to Sonic." A loud gasp. One of your teammates faints. The captain approaches you. There is death in his eyes. His hand reaches out to you. Will he slap you? Will he kill you? He holds your shoulder. Then he says, "We GOTTA go to Sonic. You don't have to sit at the restaurant! You just eat in your car! Also, have you seen their ads? It's two guys in a car . . . um . . . but funny."

And that's how you all decide to go to Sonic. And here's the thing about Sonic: it is impossible to have a bite or two at Sonic. The menu is overwhelming. So many options! They have a whole section just for a series of products called "Sonic Rechargers with Red Bull," which sounds less like a drink and more like Chinese knockoff Power Rangers. Add to that a bajillion options of tots, fries, chips, onion rings, burgers . . . It's so, so much. So, you ate A LOT. Like burgers, and tots, and fries, and shakes, and you guys were NOT feeling well the night before the big game. Or the day of the big game. Or during the big game. And you lost.

At the end of the season, the coach says you won't be punished for the Sonic incident, but the team has agreed to send you to another team. You notice how in the United States they don't say you're being "sold," which is what they say everywhere else in the soccer world. Because in America we don't sell people. Anymore. The next team is Montreal Impact/Impact Montréal.

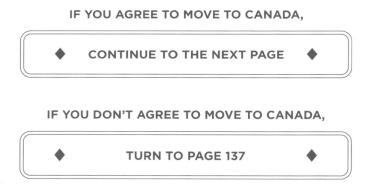

IF YOU AGREE TO MOVE TO CANADA,

◆   **CONTINUE TO THE NEXT PAGE**   ◆

IF YOU DON'T AGREE TO MOVE TO CANADA,

◆   **TURN TO PAGE 137**   ◆

◆

YOU AGREE TO MOVE TO CANADA.

And what luck! You get off the Air Canada plane at Montreal's Pierre Trudeau International Airport, the only airport in the world named after a zaddy's daddy. Unfortunately, you can't read the signs in French and crash through a glass door. Also because they are in Québécois French, so even if you did speak French you wouldn't want to read them on principle. A shard lodges into your knee and you're out for the season. But you're in Canada! Health care is free. After a year, you're back in action, and since you're not a hockey player, you get to live the life of an athlete but without the crazy level of fame where people stop you on the street.

You jump around teams in Canada, meet a wonderful man named Ryan, and retire from professional soccer at 31. You marry Ryan in a ceremony in Colombia and become a personal trainer in his hometown of Calgary. The money you made from your professional soccer career allows you to open a car dealership, and after that a couple of Tim Horton's franchises. You wonder if you'd picked a different life, maybe you'd own your own chain of donut restaurants named after you and not after a hockey player you never met.

But you didn't become the next Maradona or the next Pelé, or even the next Gareth Barry,* but when you play with your kids, they say you're the best soccer player in the world. And you believe it.

THE END

---

*For the Americans reading this book, Gareth Barry is to English football what Miles Plumlee is to basketball: an okay player whose name makes you say, "Oh, right! Him!"

♦

YOU DON'T AGREE TO MOVE TO CANADA.

You remain a bench player at Columbus Crew. You play until you're the oldest player on the team at 35. At this point, you have been working in the United States for so long, you have been able to acquire a green card. But your story is not over yet! See, even if you have a green card, your immigration story is never truly over. Continue reading to learn about the labyrinth that is applying for a green card through your job.

EB-1 VISA/ GREEN CARD

This is basically an O-1 visa for extraordinary ability's Pokémon Evolution. This is the visa you get when you want to tell the government, "Yeah, I'm hot shit." And you know what? You are. Because it's a green card, which is a colloquial name for a Permanent Resident Card, and it means that once you have it, you never have to re-apply for a visa again. It certifies that you live here. Legally. No ifs, ands, or buts. As long as the far-right does not get into power, in which, best case, you will be deported, and worst case, you'll be absorbed by Stephen Miller's nutrient sac.

The EB-1 visa is a green card made available for immigrants with extraordinary ability—but that includes everyone from artists and creatives, outstanding professors, and even managers and executives. It's about time high-earning executives had something good happen to them. All you must do to get it is prove your extraordinary ability. And the best part? There's no quota or cap. America will accept as many super-extraordinary teachers/artists/CEOs as it wants.

However, because of that, it has a much higher rejection rate than other visas. For example, the approval rate for an O-1 was 91.4 percent in 2021, whereas about 50 percent of EB-1 applications get approved. So, pretty much a coin toss! Your future and permanence are at the mercy of George Washington, or whatever the state quarter for Wisconsin has on the tails side. Is it cheese? Of course it's cheese. It's Wisconsin. It's cheese and a crossed-out picture of Aaron Rodgers.

There are three EB-1 subcategories.

1. EB-1A: Extraordinary Ability; i.e., The Einstein Visa, named after famed astrophysicist, Albert Visa.

The USCIS says, "You must be able to demonstrate extraordinary ability in the sciences, arts, education, business, or athletics through sustained national or international acclaim." The hard part here is "sustained." So, you gotta be working like Tom Hanks or Judy Greer. You have to be booking. If you only have one IMDb credit, you're out.

You don't need to have an offer of employment to get this green card as long as you show evidence that you will be working within the industry list on your application. (Don't apply for an EB-1 as a consultant if you are a painter.) The requirements are the O-1 requirements, but *harder*. Also, you don't need to have an immediate job offer for this one! Hee hee! Come here and mooch, artists!

What are the requirements? Pretty insane, just like the O-1, but the government has a higher bar for an EB-1 than an O-1. For example, instead of asking for just awards, they recommend that you apply as a winner of a "globally acclaimed award" from a list that includes a Pulitzer, an Oscar, or an Olympic medal. If you have won all three: congratulations. You get to be president. Except you can't. You weren't born here (that was a trick question!). God, this immigration system is so confusing!

If you don't have one of these measly awards, USCIS wants you to have at least THREE of the following TEN requirements:

- Evidence of "lesser nationally or internationally recognized prizes or awards for excellence." So, less Emmy Award and more J.D. Power Award for best midsized sedan.
- Evidence of "membership in associations in the field which demand outstanding achievement of their members." So, if there's a Big Nerds Club in your country, join it!
- Evidence of "published material about you in professional or major trade publications or other major media." So get in the newspapers! But for good

reasons only. They do NOT give out EB-1s for "Man Barges into Sunglass Hut Naked Riding Horse. Horse Is Pressing Charges."

- Evidence that you have been asked to "judge the work of others, either individually or on a panel."
- Evidence of "original scientific, scholarly, artistic, athletic, or business-related contributions of major significance to the field." For example, you invented a way to do surgery, or a specific form of capitalist exploitation, or the phrase "Cowabunga!"
- Evidence that you wrote "scholarly articles in professional or major trade publications or other major media."
- Evidence that your work has been displayed at artistic exhibitions or showcases.
- Evidence of your performance of a leading or critical role in distinguished organizations.
- Evidence that you command a high salary or other significantly high remuneration in relation to others in the field.
- Evidence of your commercial successes in the performing arts. Local productions of *A Christmas Carol* don't count. They don't care if you played all the parts.

You can apply by yourself if you hate yourself. Otherwise, just fork out about ten grand for a lawyer. Your wait time is about six months, but it could also be more because fuck you, that's why. If you pay $2,500 for premium processing, you'll hear back in two weeks.

2. EB-1B: Outstanding Professors and Researchers, i.e., NEEEEEERRRRRRDDDSSSS!

The USCIS asks applicants to prove they have "international recognition for [their] outstanding achievements in a particular academic field." So, if you're one of those scholars who's dedicated all her life to one line in the Decameron, you're in luck. Also, I'd love to introduce you to the concept of television.

They also say you *must* have at least three years of experience teaching or researching in that academic area, and that you must come to the US to teach or research. They specifically ask you to come here to pursue tenure or tenure-track teaching or a comparable research position at an American university, institution of higher education, or private employer. So, a little easier for scientists who could work in research for a private company. A little harder for humanities professors. Hey, maybe Amazon is looking for baroque-opera professors.

Applicants must also meet two of the six criteria below:

- Evidence of receipt of major prizes or awards for outstanding achievement. Homecoming king/queen does *not* count.
- Evidence of membership in associations that require their members to demonstrate outstanding achievement.
- Evidence of published material in professional publications written by others about the noncitizen's work in the academic field. So, basically, get your teacher friends to talk about how good you are in their own work. For example, right now I'm gonna reference some cool scientists who weren't born here: Marie

Curie (Poland), Dr. Siddhartha Mukherjee (India), Dr. Brian Cox (England), Doctor Who (Gallifrey? But according to new canon, maybe not?).

- Evidence of participation, either on a panel or individually, as a judge of the work of others in the same or allied academic field.
- Evidence of original scientific or scholarly research contributions in the field.
- Evidence of authorship of scholarly books or articles (in scholarly journals with international circulation) in the field.

Unlike for an EB-1A, you do need to have a job offer for this visa, and your employer needs to show their accomplishments and that they employ at least three full-time researchers. So, you can't just get a job at Papa John's. However, you *can* get a job as part of the research team that creates the liquid cocaine that is Papa John's garlic sauce.* Your employer also has to prove that they can pay your wage by disclosing financial information. You cannot apply for this visa yourself. Your US employer must file a Form I-140, Petition for Alien Worker. So, in the previous example, Papa John himself has to apply for you.

Kevin again. So, obviously Papa John's garlic sauce is not made out of liquid cocaine. Cocaine cannot exist in liquid form and also, there is no scientific way of truly knowing what goes into Papa John's garlic sauce.

3. EB-1C: Multinational Managers or Executives—
"The most beautiful, smartest people in the world."

This is one of those applications where the USCIS does a riddle. They say, "You must have been employed outside the United States for at least 1 year in the 3 years preceding the petition or the most recent lawful nonimmigrant admission if you are already working for the US petitioning employer." Adding, "Also, you must enter the United States via boat crossing a river. Next to you are a sack of grain, a chicken, and a fox. You can only carry one at a time. Why can't the doctor operate on him?"

At the same time, they say that "The US petitioner must have been doing business for at least 1 year, have a qualifying relationship to the entity you worked for outside the US, and intend to employ you in a managerial or executive capacity." So, you can't just start a company called Fernando Inc. and call yourself president. You have to start a company called Fernando Inc. in your own country, then open Fernando International in the United States, operate it for a year, and then name yourself president. Easy peasy, right?

You can't apply for this one on your own either. Your US employer must request your residence and prove they can afford to pay you. Sorry, America doesn't want broke bitches.

FILING FEES

$700

Employment Sponsor Fee: **$260**

Legal Fees: **Upwards of $10,000**

After twelve years in the city, you are now a local in Columbus. You live in a perfectly nice neighborhood with perfectly nice people. You've met the love of your life, an English teacher named Tristan. One night, you're having dinner with your neighbors, Jim and Alison. Jim owns a data analytics company and Alison . . . owns the biggest house on the block. They cannot wait to tell you about the trip they're taking next summer: an all-inclusive cruise to "Far Asia." You're surprised anyone still calls it "Far Asia."

"We're going to China," John says. "But it's so much paperwork," interrupts Alison. "Can you believe we have to get a visa?" And you say, yes. You can believe it. And they catch themselves, which prompts John to say, "Oh, but this is different. We're not *moving* there. We're just visiting." You tell them people from your country need to get a visa just to visit the United States. And then Alison says, "Well, that's because of all the people coming here to stay. Not you. You're one of the good ones." And right there you feel it: the wrath of every *muisca* native from the plains of Bogotá who died of smallpox because some conquistador didn't wash his sheets. It rises from the pit of your stomach all the way up to your limbs. Your brain is a chant in a native language you do not speak but have always known. You want to tell her that there are no good ones or bad ones. That she's just lucky she happened to be born here in this big plot of land that was stolen by guys in buckle hats. That borders are stupid. That laws keep changing. That Alison and John's grandparents came here when laws didn't restrict immigration in the same way as they do now. Or they did but only when white people decided they randomly hated other kinds of white people because they were too Catholic or too loud or had too many consonants in their last names. You want to tell her she is an ignorant idiot. That she shouldn't speak about something she doesn't know anything about. But that you know she must, because that's what makes her American. You want to tell her that you hope the Chinese deny their visa, that they'll have to watch everyone else go have fun in Shanghai while they're stuck on the boat with a warm pile of shrimp cocktail. You want to tell her the steak they served you is overcooked. That their house is an eyesore. That data analytics is boring. That you're so angry, but mostly at yourself, because you thought they wouldn't be like this, but then you remember there are so many people like this. And nothing you say is going to change their minds, but you're going to say it anyway. You're going to say that you're leaving. But you don't have to. Because before you can say a word, your sweet Tristan says, "Alison, that's an incredibly ignorant thing to say." And then he calmly explains why they're morons in that cute little Ivy League grad tone he has. He's destroying them in his own house. Using his own language. Not ever raising his voice. He's reminding you he's not like them. He's one of the good ones.

THE END

◆

YOU HAVE NOT SECRETLY BEEN AN ELITE-LEVEL ATHLETE THIS WHOLE TIME.

No, you are not an elite-level athlete. You stare at the computer screen, mouth agape, for a few minutes. "It seems like your lawyer applied for an O-1A visa." This person is a professional. Her job is to know immigration law. And she applied for the wrong kind of visa. You have to agree with the US government. You do not qualify for that kind of visa. You have to agree with her. Maybe that's why she insisted you weren't getting the visa. As baffling as this is, this is the truth about being an immigrant. Your life is never in your own hands. It is an emotional rollercoaster that's also a Ferris wheel of the heart and a crazy teacups ride of feelings. What these heavily constructed metaphors imply is that you constantly feel like you want to throw up.

You inform the ad agency you will no longer be using the mean lawyer they provided. The HR/legal/payroll woman asks you to please draft an email where you explain why the company will not be using her services anymore, you assume because this boutique agency is going to try and ask for a refund. You draft the email. A couple of times. You are a copywriter, but it's still pretty hard to find the right way to politely say "Are you fucking kidding me?" The final draft you send to the company is still considered too angry for the company, and they end up getting another copywriter to give it another pass. That copywriter is married to an immigrant, and while he does tone down the letter, he also buys you a beer that evening.

Your new lawyer, who is your old lawyer, collects your documents and you re-file a petition with the USCIS. This time, you apply as an Alien of Extraordinary Ability in the Arts. That means he has applied for an O-1B visa.

WHAT IS AN

O-1B VISA?

If you are an artist and might just have what the government calls "extraordinary ability in the arts or extraordinary achievement in motion picture or TV industry," then you may qualify for an O-1B visa. This, too, is a three-year visa, that can be extended in one-year increments or reapplied to for additional three-year periods.

What do you need to qualify? Well, if you don't have a one-time major distinction (Academy Award, Director's Guild Award, Pulitzer Prize) you need to have at least three of the following:

- You've been the lead in a production or an event that is recognized by reviews, ads, or PR releases. So, never get mad at your mom for saving clippings of you and your little improv shows in the local paper. Get mad that she hasn't sent them to the government.

- You've been the lead and will continue to be the lead or play a critical role for organizations that have been recognized as evidenced by reviews, ads, or PR releases. So, maybe that ad you wrote where Chris Pratt shares a Michelob Ultra with Godzilla hasn't appeared in the "best ads of this year's Super Bowl." But maybe the agency you write for is famous for making great ads, and Michelob Ultra is a huge brand. That can help.

- You have national and/or international recognition in your field as recognized by reviews or other published materials. Time to call your dad's friend who worked at that magazine. And that guy you went to college with who interned at that blogging website. And literally anyone who can write anything nice about you as an artist.
- Do you have major commercial or critically acclaimed success? For example, are you "Baby"-era Justin Bieber? If you are "Baby"-era Justin Bieber, you will probably qualify for an O-1B.*
- Have your achievements been recognized by organizations, critics, government agencies in the US or in your country, or by other experts in your field? If you can prove it, that could help your case.
- Once again, dolla dolla billz.

*Other eras of Justin Bieber may also qualify.

What comes next will be some of the most stressful months of your life. As much as you feel confident that you have enough evidence, and as nice as your lawyer and his staff are about your chances, there is no way of knowing if your visa will be approved. Since this lawyer is not terrible at his job and is also kind to you, you feel like you can actually ask questions. This lawyer explains a little bit more about the visa process. He tells you that the people who ultimately make the call about your visa are civil servants who sometimes only have a high school education. They are also not paid incredibly well, and their job and the way they perform it can sometimes be at the whims of the current administration. When you're applying, President Obama is still in office. The next time you apply, he won't be, and somehow the haunted process of putting your life in the hands of a stranger will be even more cursed.

This lawyer also tells you that getting premium processing might make it more likely you get another RFE, so that it's best if you just wait for the longer processing time. You don't really question why, but this is one of those things you will learn throughout this process: there are quirks and rules and trapdoors that spring and change places all the time. USCIS starts "asking for more of X" or "looking more closely at Y" or "taking longer with Z" just because, and the only way to find out about these things is by talking to immigration lawyers or other immigrants who are going through this whole process. As of the writing of this book, I don't know if this thing I heard from another immigrant is still true. But it was at the time. And it is a fact that lives in my head. And it's incredibly alienating to hold all this information in your brain when your friends in America who are American never have to learn these things. This is another one of the things that the immigration system does to you—it makes you memorize all these rules when you could be using your brain to memorize more important things, like birthdays or poems or the lyrics to "We Didn't Start the Fire."

The problem with not getting premium processing is that the process then takes months, and your OPT will expire while you're waiting for your result. That doesn't mean you'll be staying in the country illegally, but it does mean that if the government says no, you must leave as soon as you hear the "no." You also begrudge how many acronyms you've had to learn because of immigration: USCIS, RFE, OPT. TMI, amirite? GTFO with that BS. WTF? Just issue the visa, USA! WWJD!!! J would def IAV (Issue A Visa) and he'd add some L&Fs (Loaves & Fishes) on the side.

You spend the next couple of months trying simultaneously to think about and not think about your visa. It is impossible to live your life thinking it is very likely that you will have to leave the life you have worked very hard to build. You keep doing improv, you keep writing, you keep going on dates, because you can't just wait in stasis if everything goes south. But it is hard to enjoy the things you do, because if everything does go south, *you* will have to go south. To your native Colombia.

You try not to think that even if your visa is approved, it's not actually approved until you get it stamped on your passport. Even if the government tells you that it's okay and you got the visa, they're not issuing you a visa. They are issuing you a notice of approval. After you get it, you need to return to your home country to get it stamped on your passport. At the embassy. And just like with every other visa, the final decision is at the discretion of one person behind the glass. This seems like an unnecessary hassle, but that's the magic of the immigration process. It's *all* unnecessary hassle. And yes, if the embassy officer rejects your visa at the embassy, that is it. You can't come back to the United States. It's kinda wild to think your entire life is in the hands of one person who might've just woken up in a bad mood or gone on a bad date or is just mad at their boss because they did something dumb like making you write an email they could've written, or something truly evil and despicable like scheduling a meeting on a Friday at 4:30 p.m. on a day when you didn't have that much to do and you had all agreed you were going to Chili's.* But if you take too long to think about how your entire life is in the hands of a normal human whose actions might be dictated by their irrational thoughts, you'll go nuts or at least start thinking your dog can talk to you and is telling you you need to go on *American Idol* so you can marry Katy Perry.

Technically, you don't have to go to your own country to get the visa stamped. You just need to go to a US embassy anywhere in the world. You start to consider whether you could take a sneaky little vacation. Maybe a short *aventura* in Mexico City. Or a *sojourn* in Paris. Or a drive up to Ottawa? No, no. That fate is too cruel. However, your lawyer, and other lawyers later, will tell you not to go get the visa stamped at the London embassy. Apparently, they love to reject visas after approval. No one knows why, but the people at the London embassy are meaner. Probably because they have to live in London.

---

*In this scenario, there is a Chili's close to the embassy where the officer works. I don't know all the US embassies in the world, but I do know that the only Chili's in Colombia is right next to the US embassy, which feels like that Chili's is part of the embassy and technically US territory. So let's pretend this scenario happens there.

It is during this time of uncertainty that you will meet that girl you will eventually marry.

TO ASK HER OUT ON A DATE,

◆ TURN TO PAGE 158 ◆

TO NOT ASK HER OUT ON A DATE,

◆ TURN TO PAGE 156 ◆

◆

YOU DO NOT ASK THE GIRL YOU WILL
EVENTUALLY MARRY ON A DATE.

The title of this section poses a philosophical question. This book is, in a sense, Calvinist, which, as a person who was raised Catholic, makes the author feel iffy. You are predestined to be the characters in the paths presented in this book. It presents the illusion of free will, but you are still limited by the options and decisions that are in the book. Since most of the stories in the book are fake but based on reality, that doesn't really matter too much. But this particular story you've been following is real and based on the author's life. So, by choosing to not do what the author did, you are rebelling against the author. Which is very rude of you. I mean, do you think you're better than me? Have you even written a book? I mean, I guess you may have written a book. Well, you still have to do whatever I say because you are reading MY book. HAH! I am in control here. I AM A GOD HERE. You may *think* you're better than me, but *I* can make you think whatever I want you to think! Because you're gonna think what I write! Elephant! Rhinoceros! Your parents' divorce was your fault! Haha! I made you think of that. Take that, ya chump! Wait, I'm so sorry I called you a chump. And that I said that thing about your parents' divorce. I don't even know if your parents are divorced. I'm sorry. Thank you for buying this book, or at least for reading it . . . Wow. Having unlimited power turned me into a real asshole. Would you turn into a giant douche if *you* had unlimited power? Maybe you *are* better than me. I guess we both learned a lot in this section.

Anyway, you didn't ask her on a date, but the joke's on you because the girl you will eventually marry ends up asking *you* on a date. You don't know that now, but after you marry her, she will tell you that if you hadn't asked her on a date, she would've. So, take that! There is no free will in this book! But hey, you get to be very happy with a person who truly loves you so . . . could be worse!

THE END

◆

YOU ASK THE GIRL YOU WILL EVENTUALLY
MARRY ON A DATE.

You go on a date with that girl who was mentioned earlier. The one who likes the letter of recommendation written by your favorite writer. And that will be a problem, because dating experts agree that falling quickly and madly in love with someone when you don't know if, within a month after your first date, that someone will still be living in the same geographic area is a major turn off. You may be surprised to learn this but leaving the country by order of the United States Citizenship and Immigration Services, with no clear knowledge of if and/or when you will be able to return, has never been included in *Cosmo*'s Top 10 Tips That Will Drive Him Wild.

You meet her in improv class, which is embarrassing. There is no other way around it. It is only *slightly* more dignified than saying you met her at clown college or at a Nickelback concert. Fun fact: she attended a Nickelback concert once, but only so she could see the opener—Chris Daughtry. Which is even more embarrassing. You will find space in your heart to forgive her for this incredibly uncool thing. You are a forgiving and generous lover. She will find space in her heart to forgive you for pretty much every incredibly dweeby thing you have ever done, like knowing every single word to Galadriel's prologue in *The Lord of the Rings: The Fellowship of the Ring* and insisting on reciting it WHILE she watches the movie with you. You've already won, dude. She's watching the movie with you. Don't mess it up. She will also forgive you for going Dutch on your first date. In your defense, you're still not making much money. Also, that is no defense. That is a bad thing to do.

Your first date is in a French restaurant in Harlem. You each have three beers and you only share an appetizer of fried calamari. Why? You're both broke and you both want to seem cool and not bothered about the fact that the restaurant you both picked is way above your budget. It is very easy to talk to her. She wants to know everything about you, and since your visa has been the only thing on your mind for months now, you start blabbering about it like a five-year-old describing his Pokémon cards to a very confused grandparent. But she's into it. She wants to know more. She wants to hear about your lawyers—the good and the bad. She wants to understand why it's so hard for someone to just . . . be here. That's why you show her the letter. She says, "Oh, wow. That's cool." And you like that, for the first time since you started dating, someone isn't saying that about the fact that you write listicles for a website. At the end of the date, you walk her home. You have made it clear that any day you may hear back from the government and disappear. She still kisses you goodnight when you drop her off at her stoop. Full tongue. Score. You walk home and, for a few hours, you actually don't think about the visa.

You go on one more date before you each leave New York for the holidays. She goes home to Kansas City, while you go to spend Christmas with your cousins in Allentown, Pennsylvania. That sounds depressing, but it's actually very nice. Shout-out to Allentown. While you're there, you go with your four cousins (three of them teens), your aunt, your uncle who was born in Iraq, and your grandmother to buy a Christmas tree. It's the first time a lot of these Colombians are buying a real Christmas tree. It's so quintessentially American. After you pick the tree and get it wrapped, and after the nice people who work there wish you a merry Christmas and help load the tree onto the car, you notice the sign in the window of the farmhouse. It is bright red with white letters. It reads, "Make America Great Again." You wonder if they will ever know that they just served a family of Colombian/Iraqi immigrants.

When you get home, you receive an email from your lawyer. Your O-1B petition has been approved. You will, finally, be able to work as a writer in the United States for three years. After that, you can apply for one-year renewals every year pretty much forever, which is cool, until you think about it for a second and then it is less cool and more . . . how do you say . . . Sisyphean. You feel like your arms are made of pudding and your legs are made of jelly and your head is made of whatever Flubber was made of. Sentient goo? You have no idea what will come next. You may actually be able to get on those house teams at that improv theater you perform and train at. You may get a job at another ad agency, and then another, and then another, until you're aching to leave the ad world because you know that while you could make a career out of it, all you want to do is write funny stuff. You might work at *The Daily Show* like you imagined. Or maybe a smaller show, to start. Or maybe you will be so lucky, so incredibly fortunate, that you will get your first television job writing for the biggest late-night show in the country. Hah! Who could ever be so lucky? And maybe that job will be so rewarding, and you will learn every single day from your bosses and your coworkers.

And maybe you will feel empowered to tell your stories in your writing. And maybe you will write a book about immigration. And it will be silly, but it will be good. It will be so good; the book will win the Academy Award for Best Picture. They don't even give Academy Awards to books, but this book will be *that* good. And the person reading that book will be the smartest, most beautiful person in the world. And maybe you will find so many friends, born in the US and born abroad. And they will make you laugh, and they will love you so much that they will visit Colombia for your wedding just to show you how much they love you. Maybe you will find love. Maybe you've already found it. There's no way of knowing if these things will happen. All you know is that you're going to call your mom. And you're going to cry a little. And maybe text that girl.

THE END

♦

YOU ARE A DEMIGOD AMONG MERE MORTALS.

Whoa, you're tall! Also, you're from Slovenia. Although, when you were born it was still Yugoslavia. Isn't it funny how nations, borders, and nationalities are manmade constructs that are constantly changing? Not funny like a joke that makes you laugh, or that viral video of the newscaster who gets headbutted by a goat, but that kind of serious funny that makes you go "hah." And then you congratulate yourself for finding it funny. Like a *New Yorker* cartoon or a Danish movie that is referred to as a comedy but has zero scenes of Will Ferrell taking his shirt off.

You live in the capital city of Ljubljana, or, as it's commonly known, Europe's most consonantiest place! In college, at the University of Ljubljana, or, as one assumes it's known there, Ljunjivjerstjy ojf Ljubljana, you enter a modeling competition, and you win! The grand prize is an international modeling contract, which actually comes through and isn't some weird scam. That means you drop out of the university. Who njeeds a djipljoma, anyway?

After a few successful years in Europe during which you pose for glamorous international magazines like *Vogue*, *GQ*, and *Harper's Bazaar*, you travel to Paris, where you meet Paolo Zampolli, an Italian *impresario*, which is Italian for "impressive dude"!* Zampolli owns a company called ID Models, which has established itself as a leading modeling company in the United States. He says he will sponsor you, so you'll be able to leave Europe and move to and work in the US.† You don't have to think about it. You're not just leaving Europe—you're leaving Slovenia. A former Yugoslavian country. A country that was and is still at war. And you're leaving it for America.

It is important to remember the impact that the United States had on the world in the early 1990s. Even today, with school shootings

---

*It's not.

† As the author, I'm going to take a second for a brief aside on this guy. Unlike a lot of the characters introduced in this book, Paolo Zampolli is a real guy. I included him for two reasons. The first one is that he's super weird. As of the writing of this book, Zampolli has become the ambassador to the United Nations from the Caribbean nation of Dominica. Is he from Dominica? Nope. Does he live there? Nope. He is unmarried and his longtime partner is a model but also an ambassador to the UN, but not for Dominica. She's an ambassador for Grenada, which is another Caribbean island-nation. I have no idea why they are the ambassadors to the UN from countries they are not from. I guess that's very United Nations of them. Also, Zampolli's website only features a picture of himself holding a globe in one hand, while his other hand is gently placed on the shoulder of a child wearing a little suit. The child also has a globe. Over the picture are the words "Ambassador Paolo Zampolli." There's nothing else on the website. It's just weird. Also, when Henry Kissinger died, Zampolli posted a photo of himself with Kissinger on his Instagram, and in the caption, he let it slip that he has Delta Million Miler status. He is SO weird. The other reason I included him is because he lives in New York, so he's another immigrant. So there ya go: here's a bonus immigrant story in this book. *De nada.*

and the ever-increasing threat of the death of democracy, millions of people want to move to America. Imagine the grip this country had on the world in 1993. *Jurassic Park* had just come out. Anything is possible. They made dinosaurs real. Not really, but they looked pretty real. They still look pretty real today, and it's been over thirty years. So, you don't think twice and say yes to Paolo. He tells you you'll have to apply for a modeling visa.

HOW TO MODEL IN THE UNITED STATES

If you want to model in the United States, my beautiful assistant can show you two paths behind two mystery doors!

Hi, I'm Carly. I'm the beautiful assistant, but also so much more than that. I also have a degree in biochemistry from Rutgers. Also, I enjoy baking and the music of Fleetwood Mac and Kendrick Lamar. On Saturdays, I play laser tag with my friends.

Show them what's behind door number one, Carly!

Okay, but because I want to. Not because you ordered me to.

O-1 Visas for Fashion Models
If you're a model, you can also apply for an O-1B visa because you have extraordinary ability in the art of fashion. Yes, fashion is art. It has all the defining characteristics of art: it's pretty to look at, it's expensive to own, it gives people joy, and it's mostly run by white guys.

To successfully obtain an O-1B for modeling, applicants must present slightly different evidence than other artists would, which should include but not be limited to:

- Magazines. With you on the cover or gracing its pages in any way. Do not give your old, unread *New Yorker* issues to the government.
- Runway photos. (1) Because they show you working, and (2) because they show America you can join the military and are ready to *serve*.
- Press. Clips, interviews, magazine covers, appearances in local media. Hey, if you modeled for Belarus's equivalent of the Sears catalog, it counts. Belarus's version of the Sears catalog is of course titled *Capitalist Rag for Very Much Kindling Young Man Sexuality and Also Gardening.*
- Advertisements. If you're the face of a product, we wanna see that. Even if you are the unfortunate person whose picture was used for a brand of adult diapers. No, you don't need them, but a gig is a gig is a gig is a gig.

- Awards. I honestly didn't know they gave out awards for modeling, so here's a list I made up: Best Thin. Most Tall. Most Not-Thin in a Way That Is a Statement. Outstanding Performance in Cheekbones.
- And, as always, high compensation rate. America can be bought, babyyyyy.

Of course, this is in addition to the other things required to apply for an O-1, which are enumerated on page 118.

Great. Now *if you want to*, could you show the readers what's behind door number two?

Hmmm. Now, I don't want to, but I will do it because it's my job and I am a fricking professional.

H-1B3 Visas for Fashion Models

The only visa that sounds like a *Star Wars* droid!

The USCIS will issue certain kinds of H-1B foreign worker visas for models. However, they specify that these only count for jobs or services that "require a fashion model of prominence." So not the Belarusian Sears catalog? But maybe yes? What if you said you're the hand model for the iPhone 6S? Who's even gonna check? Well, like a regular H-1B visa, this job has to first be certified by the Department of Labor. But if Apple wants to hire you to be the eye model for their brand-new Apple Retinal Implant That Tells You Your GrubHub Is Here Plus Max, and they think your retinas are the only ones that are good enough to convince other people to sign up, they can tell that to the Department of Labor.

Once the position has been approved by them, the petitioner (i.e., the company) must prove to the USCIS the following:

- The model is prominent in the industry—the fashion industry, that is. They do not care if you are the number one fishmonger in Poland.
- The model has a higher degree of skill and fame than normal fashion models; this is your chance to tell your professional rivals that you're literally better than them. Take it.
- The model has been offered a job that involves distinguished events or productions (think BMW's new car launch, not Crazy Mike's 24-Hour Carwash and Pet Groomers in Olathe, Kansas).
- The model has been offered a job that involves entities that are distinguished. (So definitely a billionaire's party, but maybe not the billionaire's orgy after.)
- The model will be paid a wage rate that is higher than what US workers in similar jobs in the same geographic area would make. (Know your worth, girl. Then tell the government about it.)

As with all H-1B visas, models who apply for the H-1B3 must apply for the H-1B lottery. Look, you may be pretty, but we're not gonna let you just walk in. It's the only way to prevent all our brave CBP officers from seeing you and then going "AOOOOOOGA" as their heads transform into a wolf's and their eyes pop out of their sockets.

◆

YOU ARRIVE IN AMERICA ON A VISITOR OR A TOURIST VISA.*

But since you're definitely gonna get your modeling visa that allows you to work, who cares if you do a few gigs on that visa? Truly, who cares? Technically it's illegal for you to work on a tourist visa, but . . . sincerely, who is getting hurt? If you're a model, they're picking you because of *your* looks. For the most part, this thought can be translated to most cases of people working "illegally" in the United States. Sure, it's not allowed according to "the rule of law," but, while this book is not condoning the breaking of any laws, it is asking you to rethink or learn about immigration, and so it's a good opportunity to question the idea of many of our immigration laws. When people work in the United States without authorization, they usually are not breaking the law in any way that is breaching the so-called social contract that keeps us safe. It is important to emphasize the "keeping us safe" aspect of it all, because during George W. Bush's administration, the United States Citizenship and Immigration Services had

---

*For more information on what a tourist visa is, turn to page 99.

been a part of the Department of Homeland Security. Originally, immigration was under the jurisdiction of the Department of Labor, and later the Department of Justice. The fact that now it is a wing of Homeland Security tells us much about how immigration is perceived by the government since the turn of the twenty-first century. Immigration is now a matter of national security, which explains irrational decisions and unnecessary delays. If immigration were its own department or if it were still under the DOJ or the Department of Labor, we would regulate it in a way that would be more humane and would probably be more beneficial both to immigrants and to the economy. But since you're just a model getting modeling gigs, you can't really influence immigration policy. *Yet.*

You take at least ten modeling gigs before your work authorization comes through, but no one will find out about that until much later. Also, no one cares now, and no one will really care then. Your career really takes off in the United States. Over the course of two years, you appear in many prestigious magazines, like *Sports Illustrated* and on the cover of *InStyle*, *New York* magazine, *Vanity Fair*, and even on a billboard in Times Square with Joe Camel. One day, on your way to a shoot, you walk through Times Square. You stand below the billboard where you're smoking a cigarette. It's the late '90s. The world will never be better. And you're paving the way for other great women to have their face on giant billboards in Times Square. Women like Keira Knightley and the Green M&M. You're making a positive impact. This will be important to you during the rest of your life. You will focus on not just being but being the best version of you that you can be. Not just on *being*, but on being *best*.

During your modeling gigs in the US, Paolo introduces you to this guy he does business with. He's larger than life. His name literally is placed outside of buildings all over the country. He's married, but when has that ever stopped a man whose name is written in gold letters outside of buildings? He's getting divorced and he asks you if you want to date him.

IF YOU WANT TO DATE THE BUSINESS MOGUL,

TURN TO PAGE 172

IF YOU DO NOT WANT TO DATE THE BUSINESS MOGUL,

TURN TO PAGE 175

◆

YOU WANT TO DATE THE BUSINESS MOGUL.

You don't go on just one date with him. You go on many dates with him. You appear onstage when he declares his candidacy as president for the Reform Party in the year 2000. You don't really care about politics in this country, but he takes you out to parties, buys you jewels, dresses you up like a doll, and brags to his friends about how hot you are. It's excessive, it's opulent, it's America.

In 2005, you and the mogul get married. You marry at a church in Florida and have a reception at his estate in Florida. You have never dated someone with an estate. Who'da thunk that a young woman from the former Yugoslavia would end up with someone who owns an estate? Your wedding is attended by all the fancy people you've met in this country: Katie Couric; Matt Lauer; Rudy Giuliani; Heidi Klum; Shaq; Barbara Walters; Simon Cowell; Hillary Clinton and her cheating husband, Bill; and Regis. Organizing the seating chart is a nightmare. You can't sit Shaq at the same table as Barbara Walters; he hates her ever since she beat him in a dunking competition in 1999. During the reception, Billy Joel serenades the crowd with "Just the Way You Are," and you look around the room. You're so happy. There are so many people whose names you know there. So many people you know. So few friends.

The next year, you have his baby. He already has other kids, but this one is yours. Your only. He's not really there after the birth. He has work. Events to attend. A reality show to host. And sure, he does have to do that. But you also know he's doing other things. Like getting slapped by a porn star with a rolled-up magazine with his face on the cover. You look at your newborn. He already looks so much like him. But he will be different. He will be like him, but he will be yours.

The years go by. You think of leaving. As the buffoon you married sits on the toilet tweeting about how Robert Pattinson could do better than Kristen Stewart, you think that maybe you could do better too. Maybe you'll start dating that handsome head of security at Tiffany & Co. The one who works downstairs from your literal golden-cage apartment. He flirts with you, and you flirt back. But could you do better? Who are you? Who are you without him? You let him define you. If you leave him, there will be no more Tiffany & Co. No more coverage on Page Six. Would you even be able to see your son? You've seen the way he treats his former wives. Also, who cares if he cheats? Who cares if he's a terrible man? He's right about many things. He's right about that Obama guy, you think. You don't really care where he's from, but you're a white woman from the Balkans. If there's a racist bandwagon to jump on, you're very likely to jump on it.

Then, in 2015, the motherfucker runs for president. And fuck, he wins. He runs on an anti-immigrant platform. He condemns the very system that allowed you to be his wife. The same one that allowed your parents to move here once you had moved here. You try and leave, but why should you? He's given you everything. Plus, who cares if you have to be a fascist. You're already a birther and a pretty egotistical person. You're already like two-thirds of the way there. Who cares if he separates little immigrant children from their parents and locks them up in cages? Who cares if his government is so cruel and so incompetent they can't find the parents later? You don't really care, do you? They're not your kid. Plus, is it really so bad to be a fascist?

Yes. It is.

You die alone, choking painfully on your only allowed meal of the day: one pistachio. Unshelled.

THE END

◆

YOU DO NOT WANT TO DATE THE
BUSINESS MOGUL.

After you say you're busy the night he asks you out (because you genuinely are), he completely ignores you. In fact, he calls you an entitled whore, knowing you're still within earshot. He asks another model on a date, and she says yes. She'll go on to marry him and live a miserable existence with him. She'll also become first lady, but then both of them will go to jail, so bullet dodged, y'know?

Unfortunately, dating and later marrying a seemingly corrupt mogul* was a really good way to remain in the United States, and since there aren't that many moguls around, you start worrying about your ability to remain in the country. You rely on O-1 visas for

---

*Hey, Kevin again. So . . . since this is a fictional story about a fictional person who didn't go on a date with a fictional mogul, you'd think it would be fine to say he's corrupt, but there's a guy with really thin skin who might sue us if we say that, so I insist that we say he's "seemingly" corrupt. Please, I don't want anything to do with that guy. If he finds out I'm a lawyer, he might make me work for him.

almost fifteen years. Unfortunately, since you rebuffed Paolo's friend, the really nice, exclusive, high-end brand contracts have dried up. In fact, Paolo dropped you as a client, but you were able to find work at another modeling agency and work smaller gigs. You even took some acting classes in New York, and at one point did some voiceover acting in a couple of local commercials. You're the voice of Darla, the beaver mascot of the Pennsylvania lottery. But it's not easy. At one point, you're forced to go to your agent and ask him to get you a gig. Any gig. Because your current O-1 is expiring, and you need to keep status and pay rent. And that sleazy guy who asked you on a date is president now, and he's made everything harder. Your lawyer has told you that before the forty-fifth president took office, if you were granted an extraordinary talent visa, you were just assumed to "keep" that talent if you applied for a renewal. But now that that literal felon has become president, that has changed, and since your big clients have dried up, your lawyer says it's gonna be hard for you to maintain your status. That's lawyer talk for "your renewal is going to get rejected." In fact, you visit your lawyer, and they tell you, effectively, that you only have a couple of months left in the country before your visa expires. Also, that's not the end of the bad news. You agent calls you and sends you to an auto conference in Memphis.

You land in Memphis, Tennessee, on a hot summer morning. Of all the cities in Tennessee, it's the has-a-Bass-Pro-Shops-store-shaped-like-a-pyramid-est of them all. Your job is to stand next to a car for hours while tourists, weekend visitors, and people who go to car shows gawk at the car. They don't even look at you. They literally look at the car. What car is it? You don't know. It's a car. It does car things. It goes. It goes in reverse. It stops. That's it. Then, you notice a man looking at you. He really is not looking at the car. He wears a pretty nice button-down shirt and a pair of ridiculous khaki shorts, but he seems sweet. You smile, and he smiles at you. You're not really allowed to talk to people unless it's about the car, so you say,

"You know, the miles per gallon you can get on this baby is incredible."

He looks at you, befuddled. Then says, "I don't really know anything about cars."

You want to tell him you don't, either. You want to tell him you don't care. But all you can say is, "And don't get me started on the all-wheel drive model."

He looks at you like you're crazy. Probably because you sound insane. He mutters, "I'm really just here with a friend."

You're about to blurt out something about the heated seats, when you say, "I get off at five."

He smiles and says he'll come find you then.

His name is Stuart, and you agree to go on a date at your hotel bar. You worry that he's going to think you only want to meet him for sex, which you don't. He is cute, but he's not "I-want-to-just-bone-you-once cute." You're a model. You can still pretty much get any guy you want, so it's not that. He just genuinely seems nice. So, you make it very clear, as soon as he arrives at the bar still wearing the same shirt, but now wearing actual pants, that you will not sleep with him this night. He's disappointed but not in a bad way. Just in the way anyone who maybe thought there was a chance to get laid would be disappointed upon finding out there is no chance they'll get laid that night. You talk for hours. You tell him your entire life story, and he isn't just interested. He is curious. He asks you questions. Questions like, "Holy shit, Slovenia?! I don't think I could find it on a map. Can you show me where it is on my phone?" and "Whoa! You met Donald Trump? Could you tell he was a racist?" And you show him on the map, and you tell him, "No, but like, yes. Duh. Also, I'm from Slovenia, so I'm probably a little bit racist." And he says, "Hey, I'm from Tennessee. So, I think it's a tie." And you laugh. He makes you laugh too.

He's an optometrist in Nashville who drove up to Memphis for the weekend. You tell him you've never been to Nashville. He says maybe the next time you see each other, you could visit him. You say that it would be nice. And it is. You see him in Nashville a few weeks after, and a couple of weeks after that, he comes to visit you in New York. You take him to see the sights: the Statue of Liberty, the M&M's store, Top of the Rock (NOT THE EMPIRE STATE BUILDING ROOFTOP. WHY WOULD YOU GO TO THAT IF YOU CAN'T SEE THE EMPIRE STATE BUILDING FROM THE EMPIRE STATE BUILDING?). And he puts in the work too. He's googled the best burgers in the city and takes you to a place where they make a mac & cheese burger. He's so stoked about it. You don't really like mac & cheese but can't help but find his enthusiasm endearing. You also have great sex. He's a really, really great guy. The kind of guy you tell your friends about. Hell, he might be the kind of guy you tell your parents about.

On your last night together, you tell him the truth. That your visa is about to expire. You tell him it's going to be hard to stay in the country. He looks at you, and then says, "Well, look. I don't want to sound crazy, but what if we did the whole ninety-day fiancé thing?" He means you could return to your country and then he could propose to you, and you could come to America to get married here. You haven't really thought about that as a real possibility. In the past, you've joked about marrying someone for a green card, but you've never actually considered it. But you actually like Stuart. You've only just met him, but for the first time, the fact that you could marry an American feels real.

You tell him you really like him, but you need to take it slow. Of course, you want to stay in the country where you've established your career and your life, but doesn't the Elvis song say wise men say that only fools rush in? But then again, what do wise men know anyway? Three wise men thought it was a good idea to bring gold, myrrh, and frankincense to a baby. How about a freaking SNOO?* Or a freaking night nurse? Or at least a freaking bottle sterilizer? Wisdom doesn't mean practicality, I guess. Maybe it's okay to rush in? You tell Stuart that you wanna do it the right way: with a team of cameras from TLC following your every move. Hey, you learned a thing or two from the pervert reality show star you rebuffed.

You return to your native Slovenia, and you and Stuart agree to get you a K-1 fiancé(e) visa.

---

*A SNOO is a smart bassinet for babies. It's like the iPhone of bassinets. I don't have children, but I have seen my coworkers' babies on Zoom calls just completely zone out in these very cool pods that rock them very gently. It's the kind of thing they told us we would have "in the future" in those old cartoons from the '60s and '70s, but it actually delivers. Scientists, please invent more things like the SNOO and Rosie the robot from *The Jetsons*, and fewer things like social media. Thank you.

WHAT IS A
K-1 FIANCÉ(E) VISA?

A K1 visa allows a US citizen to bring their fiancé(e) here to get married, but only within ninety days. Wow, the drama! Someone should make a TV show about this! You could call it . . . *Betro-three months-ed*! According to the USCIS, the marriage "must be valid, meaning both you and your fiancé(e) have a bona fide intent to establish a life together and the marriage is not for the sole purpose of obtaining an immigration benefit." Only true-love marriages count. So, if a witch put you under a spell and your partner's kiss did not wake you up, you're NOT WELCOME.

The goal of this visa is to allow the non-US partner to come to the US and, once married, apply for permanent residency/a green card. If the immigrant fiancé(e) is already in the US legally (on an H1-B or O-1, or another status), they do not qualify for this visa. You can't just collect visas. They're immigration documents, not Pokémon cards.

The eligibility requirements are:
- One of you has to be a citizen. Of the United States. Of America. Just triple checking.

- You must get married within ninety days. So, not quite a shotgun wedding, but definitely a crossbow or early projectile ammunition technology wedding.
- Both of you are 100 percent single (no secret partners anywhere else in the world). Read also: NO DRAMA. You are allowed to have former lovers who will look you up on social media and, ten years after you've broken up, send you a LinkedIn message asking you to endorse them on their PowerPoint skills.
- The two of you have seen each other at least once within the two-year period before you file your petition. Also, you must be able to pick your partner out in a lineup.

  Fun fact: This can be waived if meeting your partner ahead of the visa "violates strict and long-established customs of your partner's foreign culture or social practice," or there is "extreme hardship to the petitioner" (such as a pandemic). Also, you can probably waive the requirement to see your fiancé if you forgot to wear your glasses for two years.

As of June 2023, the processing delays for getting a fiancé(e) visa (aka ninety-day fiancé[e]) were 16.5 months at the California Service Center and the Texas Service Center. So, get ready to plan a wedding via WhatsApp.

Also, the process once you file is . . . how to put it . . . probing (of the anal kind). It involves USCIS, the State Department, and CBP. USCIS warns that "at each stage in the process, background and security checks may be conducted on both you and your fiancé(e). This may include checks in various databases for national security, criminal history, and other information about you and your fiancé(e). These checks are conducted using fingerprints, names, or other biographic or biometric information." They know you inside and out. And they think you should definitely get that mole checked.

Step 1 with USCIS: Your American fiancé(e) will file a form asking USCIS to recognize your relationship. They may ask for further evidence to confirm your relationship. Do *not* send a sex tape. Trust me. Once they confirm, they forward your application to the National Visa Center, which forwards it to the US embassy of whichever country you are from.

Step 2 with the State Department: The US embassy/consulate gives you a visa interview. It's like a job interview, but instead of asking "What are your weaknesses?" they ask, "Have you ever been a member of a terrorist organization?"

Step 3 with CBP: Congrats! You've made it this far. The final step is convincing a Customs and Border Patrol officer that your relationship is real. As soon as you get off your flight. That's right. One guy or gal might be like, "You and him? I don't buy it." And it's all over.

Step 4: GET MARRIED WITHIN NINETY DAYS!!!

FILING FEES

$800

Wedding (in America): **Too much**

Wedding (not in America): **Out of respect for my American readers, I will not reveal the cost of getting married in another country. I like my American readers and don't want them to give up on life.**

Ⓐ You are cordially invited to the *shotgun* wedding of

FERNANDO MASCHERANO

and

ANNELIESE SCHNEIDER

Stuart arrives in Ljubljana with a whole film crew in tow to meet your parents. They are so excited to meet him. He is the man marrying their daughter, but also the way for them to leave Slovenia. Look, nothing against Slovenia, but people want to live in America. The media says so. Despite a lot of the US' issues and what the left-wing commentariat on Twitter and TikTok say, the United States is still a better place to live than A LOT of other countries. Your dad knows that Stuart lives in Nashville, so he's set up a pair of speakers that, upon Stuart's entrance to the apartment, will blast Dolly Parton.

His visit is a hit and makes for excellent reality television. He misreads signs, he doesn't speak a word of Slovenian, and he even enjoys your grandmother's famous *žganci*, a Slovenian dish described as "mush" that goes well with "sour milk." Yum! You agree to move with him to Nashville to prepare for "the big day."

Once you get there, the producers start to push you to "sound more foreign." They want you to not know what certain words are or what certain dishes are or what people in the US do for Thanksgiving (eat seven kinds of mush with a side of bland white meat). But you know these things because you've already lived here. You tell them this is not what you want to do, but they tell you it makes for good TV. Remember how Stuart looked like a moron when he didn't know what the word for "bathroom" was in Slovenian? And you say that yes, you know that's good TV, but that worked because Stuart really didn't know what the Slovenian word for "bathroom" was. That was all real. And you pretending to be someone you are not is not reality. To which they respond, "Correct. It's not reality. It's reality TELEVISION." You sigh. You were a model for years. You know you can pretend to be dumb. You made a fricking career out of it. So, you go with the flow. The good thing is, Stuart doesn't like it either, and he's super supportive. He even tells you he'd be willing to quit the TV show if you are unhappy. But you don't quit the show. You are miserable, but at least you're getting some decent money for this. It'll probably pay for the wedding. Mostly, you feel disappointed, but realize that perhaps a reality show on TLC is not going to be interested in providing viewers with a nuanced and careful view of the immigration system. They mostly want to show things like "hot woman with accent dumb" and "don't you think this schmo from the US is likely getting played?" But hey, at least with this show, people in the United States are actually learning something about their immigration system, right? They must be. Something good has to come out of this franchise that is so popular and so blasé about one of the most traumatic things a person can experience.

Your performance as Dumb Slavic Woman Who Maybe Is Only in It for the Green Card is lackluster at best. Hey, you're a model, not an actress. You finish the season, but do not become a fan favorite or anything. You get invited to one of the reunion specials in Los Angeles, and you see how much better the other people on the show are at being on the show. It's its own skill. The couples that didn't end up together have a way of treating each other like they're just coworkers and have a certain affection for one another. The couples that did end up together have found a way to turn their relationship into their brand. Stuart and you simply went on the show because you fell in love. And it is love. You wanna know how you know it's love? You ate a mac & cheese-filled burger for that man. And you'd do it any day. And that man? That man eats corn mush and sour milk every single time you go to celebrate Christmas in Slovenia. As you sit in the backseat of an Escalade the network hired for you, you look at the California sunset, muted by the tinted glass. You live here. Not in LA, but in the United States. You made New York your home, but it never felt right. You know LA is not your home, but somehow, in the backseat of this car, it does feel right. You look at Stuart. Stupid, sweet Stuart, with his receding hairline and his ever-fading Boston accent. You know that whether it's Los Angeles or Memphis or New York or Ljubljana, home is where Stuart is.

THE END

VERY HARD

Nope. We are not doing this. This is, for the most part, a humor book, and as such, I don't think it will be able to tell the stories of immigrants who have it "very hard" coming here with the respect and empathy they deserve. There are so many of them, and their stories are very sad, very true, and very much happening as you are reading this sentence. You can decide that this is a cowardly move and further proof that snowflakes have taken over comedy, and that the woke mob has ruined everything because you feel entitled to jokes about Venezuelan migrants who leave everything behind to literally walk to the United States. If so, you must be fun at parties. I assume your family doesn't really invite you to many of those these days.

I could tell you about these stories, but it wouldn't be funny. It would mostly be sad. What I can tell you is that people try very, very, very hard to come here. And they try absolutely crazy things to be able to stay here. In 2024, a pair of migrants staged a robbery to be able to qualify for a particular kind of visa that is granted to the victims of certain crimes. The problem is, a bystander saw the fake robbery occurring, and shot and killed the fake robber. Then, they all got in trouble when the police got involved. On the surface, it reads like the plot of one of the lesser Coen Brothers movies, but deep down you have to (1) celebrate the ingeniousness of these immigrants, and (2) really sit down and ask yourself how badly people want to live here. And I think that's very brave. That is one real and "funny" story about how it is to try and come here the "very hard" way, and it involves one dead person. So, I'm not going to write any more of these.

If you want to learn more about the "very hard" way to move to America, drop this joke book and go to the library. There are many, many books and reports on this and in other countries' major newspapers. And once you've read those, and read about the true hell that it is to come to America like they do, you may want to stop and ask yourself, Why do they want to come here so badly? And the answer is: because it's worth it. And because they're incredibly brave. That's no joke.

THE END

WHY EVEN MOVE TO AMERICA? A SORT-OF CONCLUSION

Hello, you've reached the end of the book. Wow, you read a whole book! Or maybe you skipped ahead. Sorry, you "paid for premium processing." That's a joke you'll get if you've read the book. If you skipped ahead, I'm sorry. I wanted to include a sort-of conclusion that addressed the main question behind all the goofy, zany, and often true stories in this book: Why even do this? Why subject yourself to this? Why go through a bureaucratic process that would give Franz Kafka a boner and a heart attack at the same time? And why move to *this* country? Why not Argentina? Or France? Or Thailand? Why do thousands upon thousands of people from all over the world choose to live in the United States every single year? So here is one immigrant's attempt at answering that.

Life in the US is not easy. In fact, many Americans say today that the American Dream is no longer possible. That might be true, but I don't think it has ever been possible. By definition, that's kind of what makes dreams *dreams*. It's the same reason for why that dream where you're running late to board a train to London from New York because you had to stop to buy the Big Macs for your travel companions, Yo-Yo Ma and your cousin, who doesn't look like what your cousin looks like in real life but is your cousin in the dream, is also impossible. First of all, because there is no train from New York to London, and secondly, because I'm pretty sure Yo-Yo Ma is more of a McChicken kind of guy. That said, I do think that people like me choose to move to America because America is—and don't cancel me—pretty good.

Could it be better? Sure! Most things can be, but as of this writing, in 2024, the United States is a decent place to live compared to several—if not most—other countries in the world. That statement does not ignore that the US is not as equitable a society as it once was for white middle-class people, nor that is has never been equitable for Black people. It does not erase the original sin of slavery and the genocide of Native Americans and the state-sanctioned massacres of people in other countries just because Henry Kissinger felt their governments were a bad hang. But, when it comes to living in a place where people feel safe expressing their opinions, whatever they are, there aren't that many places that come close. A depressing majority of countries in the world will have you jailed or killed for saying or doing something the government doesn't like. Here, they'll just let you die because you don't have employee-sponsored insurance. It's different! Slightly better. If only just. I mean, look, of course there's always Finland and Denmark. But if you moved there, you'd have to live in Finland or Denmark. Enjoy eating herring and getting constantly confused/set up with the only other person of color your neighbors know. The truth is that if you're a family fleeing political or gang violence in your country, the United States of America is a pretty great place to live. If you're a queer person, it's also a better place to live in compared to most other countries on the planet.

These are true things. It is sad that so often, marginalized groups must settle for "it's better than elsewhere," but it is true. What's scary is that all these things are becoming less true due to a very violent, very driven minority of people who think immigrant antifas are coming here to turn your *spins right-wing outrage machine wheel* gas stoves into *spins wheel* furries who will indoctrinate your children by order of *spins wheel* Bill Gates and *spins wheel* the female Colonel Sanders. But that's why it's worth fighting against that scary tide. Because I don't want the United States to become a place that people don't look forward to moving to. Plus, things feel pretty bad right now, but the United States is a really young country. We're merely in our terrible two-hundreds. We're gonna be way more cool when we turn three hundred. We're gonna get really good at Legos.

This country is often described as a Great Experiment. It's kind of enmeshed in its national identity. And the thing about experiments is that there's stuff that's gonna go wrong. And then you fix them. Or you try to. I don't think many other countries in the world consider themselves experiments. They consider themselves "glorious" or "righteous" or "Democratic but we actually mean totally undemocratic." And I think that's why people move here. Because despite its many, many mistakes, the United States historically has striven to be better. To continue to improve. To experiment and find ways to achieve better things for more people. That's a good experiment. And I don't think abandoning ship is gonna make it better. It's gonna be hard, but I don't want to leave the experiment in the crazy gun guys' hands. We're all in this chemistry class together, and I'm not going to leave this delicate experiment that could definitely explode in the hands of that guy. He has a gun!

So, as you reach the end of this book, I want to urge you to vote for candidates that make the American Experiment better. Because we can't vote, and *you* can. So even if you're not really feeling a particular candidate, or you're just not vibing with American Democracy these days, maybe do it for us? Think of one immigrant you like. Let's say Shakira or Tom Hiddleston. And cast your vote for them. Not "for" them. Vote for the guys who will make Shakira's life easier. Currently, that's the party whose entire platform isn't "I will marry the AR-15 I use to shoot antifa Mexicans."

That said, voting isn't enough. I encourage you to make the American Experiment better yourself. There are other ways to do this: You can support immigrants. Go to immigrant-owned restaurants or shop at immigrant-owned businesses. Use capitalism for good. But if you don't want consumption to be a source of your building of this so-called immigrant nation, then do other little things. Learn a new language. Literally any other language that isn't English. Even something that very few people in the world speak, like Basque. Because I promise you, somewhere in the United States there is a bustling Basque-American community, and if they find out you speak Basque, I am pretty sure you will (1) make them so happy, and (2) never have to pay for *txistorra* sausage in your life. Plus, you'll learn what *txistorra* sausage is! Or you can simply talk to immigrants. Literally talk to them. Listen to them. Befriend them. We don't bite. I promise that just because our legal classification is "alien," we won't burst out of your chest and try to eat you and the rest of your space-mining crew. And finally, learn. Learn about your own country and embrace the people who so willingly come here to make this place their home. We are so excited to be here. Really.

What I mean is, through voting and through your own actions, you can continue to make the United States the kind of country that other people want to move to. A country that gives you a little bit of an air of superiority when you travel to Europe. Let's turn the US into a place that makes people a little jealous. I guess what I'm saying is, let's all Make America Great Again. Wait, no. Not that. But let's make America a good nation.

Also, if you think this book helped you learn more about your own country and its crazy rules, give it to someone whom you think might learn something from it. By doing this, you are already helping. If you buy just *one* copy, you are helping immigrants feel understood. And if you buy a bajillion copies, you are helping one particular immigrant buy a beach house. I'm kidding, of course; I'm a millennial in the arts, so I can't even afford a *house* house.

Thank you for going on these journeys with me. You are now an immigrant in my eyes. I know it's confusing; there are just so many questions! I mean, what is the difference between an O-1A and an O-1B? Can I apply for my H-1B before applying for my LCA? What the hell is an embassy? Don't worry. I have the perfect book for you.

LIST OF
IMMIGRATION TERMS

The following is a list of terms that are used in this book that no person who is not an immigrant would even care to understand. You, however, have chosen to read this book, so now you must learn them. But don't worry. I made them funny, so there's some peanut butter on this "glossary of bureaucratic terms" pill.

Visa: A visa is a permit to allow you to enter the United States or other countries if you were not born there. There are many kinds of visas. They are passport page–sized stamps that go (surprise!) in your passport. Some countries have agreements with the US, so their citizens don't need visas to enter. The agreement tends to be, "Yeah, you guys are mostly white and rich, so you're cool."

Green Card: Technically, it's called a Permanent Resident Card, but it's *kinda* green so people call it a green card. Maybe it was greener in the past? Now it's aquamarine with dashes of red and blue. This is the card you receive once you become a permanent resident. So, it's more powerful than a visa, but less powerful than citizenship. You can't vote on a green card, but you do have to pay taxes. So you are literally the example of taxation without representation. Hey, that's pretty catchy! Someone should use it as a slogan for, like . . . a new country or a sports team.

Residency: A weird state in immigration where the government has decided it's okay for you to live here in America, but you're not yet a citizen. You can apply for citizenship. You are recognized as a person who permanently lives here, so that means you can enter and leave the country as you please.

Citizenship: You must do jury duty. And vote, while voting's still legal!

Documented: A person who has moved to the United States within the legal parameters and, as such, has the documents to prove it. Some people call them "legal immigrants," others call them "vermin who are ruining the blood of our nation." Which one of those people did you vote for?

Undocumented: A person who has done a really brave and crazy thing and come to America without the required paperwork. People often say these people should just move to America "the right way," like their grandparents did. However, back in the day "the right way" was going on a dangerous ocean journey and then answering the question "Do you have lice?" If you said no, welcome! Also, "the right way" today can often take literal decades. So, coming here "the right way" is not really a thing anymore. Especially because the journey is still dangerous, but the questions are harder, more absurd, and, perhaps worst of all, it's all much more expensive. You don't have a visa or a green card as an undocumented immigrant, but you still have to pay taxes.

USCIS: The United States Citizenship and Immigration Services is an agency. Why is it "an" agency if it actually consists of several services? Why is it grammatically incorrect? Probably because it was established under George W. Bush. It exists under the umbrella of the United States Department of Homeland Security. If that feels weird, it's because it is. Why is immigration UNDER homeland security? That presupposes that all immigrants are threats to our security, and that's just not true. Some of us just want to write our little funny books and our jokes for the TV. USCIS replaced the Immigration and Naturalization Service, which was part of the Department of Labor and later the Department of Justice. It's almost like, as a nation, we haven't really decided what role immigration plays in our country. In my opinion, it mostly means we get good restaurants. And bilingual babies, which we can all agree are really cute.

DHS: The Department of Homeland Security. A federal department of the government whose mission is anti-terrorism, border security, immigration and customs, cyber security, and disaster prevention. If it feels like there's an odd one out in there, it's probably the one that doesn't sound like the title of a network procedural. Seriously, CBS, I'll pitch you *Disaster Prevention*, starring Gina Rodriguez and Victor Garber. It will run for twenty-four seasons, and every dad in America will LOVE it. The DHS was created in response to 9/11, and as such, it turned immigration into this paranoid thing where we think everyone trying to move here is coming to getcha. As with most bad things that have happened in America in the aftermath of

9/11, it is a weird and not well-thought-out idea that is mostly bad for brown people.

CBP: Customs and Border Protection are the guys who literally guard the border. That means the physical border, as well as the guys in the booths at the airports. It's one of the largest law enforcement agencies in the world, right after the bajillion cops that all hang out at a single train station in New York City playing *Candy Crush* on their phones . . . and the largest law enforcement agency ever: the BTS Army.

ICE: Immigration and Customs Enforcement. Their job is to deport people. Sometimes they catch criminals; sometimes, under certain administrations, they deport your delivery guy. But they're not evil; they're just following orders.

Deportation: A sad thing.

Refugee: *See* courage.

Alien: *See* E.T., Baby Yoda, David Bowie.

Illegal: Arson! Murder! Driving 40 miles per hour when the limit is 35! Using the logo of an NFL team without authorization. Many things are illegal. People aren't.

RFE: Request for Evidence. This is a letter the government sends you when you apply for a visa or a green card saying "we need more information." It's the immigration equivalent of asking you for a re-do. It is absolutely terrifying.

Embassy: A fancy building in another country that is technically US territory. To go in, you get to go through TSA, but there's no duty-free inside. There's not even a Hudson News.

Consulate: Like an embassy, but smaller, and likely not located in the capital of a foreign country. It's like the embassy is Super Target and the consulate is just regular Target.

ACKNOWLEDGMENTS

Many US visas require what the government calls a "sponsor," which is essentially someone who can vouch for you and support you financially while you're in the United States. The following people are this book's sponsors:

Thank you to my incredible agent, Andrea Blatt, for making me feel like this country wanted my voice, my humor, my story, and all the other stories, including the one where I talk about sexy centaurs.

To my brilliant editor, Soyolmaa Lkhagvadorj, thank you for going on these journeys with me. Thank you for meeting with me once a month to help me stave off procrastination.

To everyone at Abrams including Zach Bokhour, Annalea Manalili, and Larry Pekarek, for making this book look stunning; and to Tobatron for literally illustrating the absurdity of the US immigration system.

Thank you to my spectacular manager, Ethan Stern, and his team at 3Arts, August and Adam. Every time we meet, I feel like I can be the best writer I can be.

Thank you to all the immigrants who helped me make this book happen: Deniz Çam, for your exhaustive research; Pratima Mani, for all the lawyer chats and the title chats; Orli Matlow, my OG immigrant collab partner; and Robin Virginie.

I am indebted to Lizzie Logan (who is a genius) for her feedback; to Asher Perlman, who always helps me find the silliest version of me; and to Kate Sidley for her help with the proposal and every step of the way after.

To Stephen Colbert and Tom Purcell, thank you for hiring me and for taking a risk on this Colombian with an encyclopedic knowledge of *Star Wars*. You made my American Dream possible.

Thank you to Michael Cruz Kayne for his NBA insights, to Caroline Lazar for telling me about the SNOO, and to everyone else at the *LSSC* crew: Delmonte Bent, Ariel Dumas, Glenn Eichler. Eliana Kwartler, Jay Katsir, Carley Moseley, Opus Moreschi, Barry Julien, Brian Fricking Stack, Steve Waltien, John Thibodeaux, and the Cowboys. There's no better way to get good at writing jokes than by doing it every single day with your friends.

To Emma Allen, for letting me disgrace the pages of *The New Yorker*, and to Chris Monks, for publishing my first humor piece, "An Open Letter to the Immigration Officer Who Confused Me for a Criminal," which is partially excerpted in this book. Thanks to Chris and Lucy Huber for letting me write jokes about immigration on *McSweeney's*. To Caitlin Kunkel for pushing me to write this book for years; you were right. I had it in me.

Also thanks to pals, collaborators, and my immigration support team: Danny Hurwitz, Jonathan Marks, Kendall Sherman, Daniel Taylor, Alex Wirth, Sasha Stewart, Reed Kavner, Mike Smith Rivera, Fabrizio Copano, and Dru Johnston. And to George Saunders for his life-changing kindness.

I want to sincerely thank my immigration lawyer, Dana Imperia, and the whole team at Green and Spiegel. I *literally* would not be here without you.

Thank you, Mom, and to David for never faltering in the belief that I could do what I do. I did the thing. I wrote a book. And it's all thanks to you. Thank you, Dad, for showing me comedy, and to Lety for joyfully tolerating my comedy bits since I was seven.

To Cachi, María, and Pablo for making me feel cool and teaching me Gen Z slang. I love you all, bet no cap. Holla, bruh. I will always be there to help you in your own journeys.

Thank you to the Namans, especially to Sammy and Yasin for letting me use your stories to create sillier ones. *Gracias a mi abuelita*, Hilda, for believing in me so much that you came to see me do improv in the basement of a bar. More than once.

To Cary, Becky, and Tess, thank you for the love and for always making me feel at home.

And to Taylor, thank you for being my wife, my companion, the petitioner of my I-130 form, and my first reader. For being there for every call with the lawyers and every JFK entry. And that one entry at Atlanta International. I only tell these stories because you constantly remind me how important it is that I do. I love you.

To all the people who leave their homes in search of a new place, thank you for being so brave.

ABOUT THE AUTHOR

FELIPE TORRES MEDINA is a Peabody and Writers Guild of America Award–winning writer from Bogotá, Colombia. His writing for *The Late Show with Stephen Colbert* has earned him five Emmy nominations. His humor has appeared in *The New Yorker*, *McSweeney's*, and others. He lives in New York City with his wife and is totally chill when you misspell his birth country's name. (He is not.)